# THE COLLECTOR'S ENCYCLOPEDIA OF
# NORITAKE

## SECOND SERIES

by
Joan Van Patten

**COLLECTOR BOOKS**
*A Division of Schroeder Publishing Co., Inc.*

The current values in this book should be used only as a guide. They are not intended to set prices, which vary from one section of the country to another. Auction prices as well as dealer prices vary greatly and are affected by condition as well as demand. Neither the Author nor the Publisher assumes responsibility for any losses that might be incurred as a result of consulting this guide.

## Searching for a Publisher?

We are always looking for knowledgeable people considered to be experts within their fields. If you feel that there is a real need for a book on your collectible subject and have a large comprehensive collection, contact us.

COLLECTOR BOOKS
P.O. Box 3009
Paducah, Kentucky 42002-3009

Cover design:  Beth Summers
Book design:  Pamela Shumaker

Additional copies of this book may be ordered from:

Collector Books
P.O. Box 3009
Paducah, KY 42002-3009

@$24.95 Add $2.00 for postage and handling.

Copyright: Joan Van Patten, 1994

# Dedication

In memory of Rita Gillis, my dear friend and mentor.

She gave me her knowledge, her support and best of all her friendship. She had confidence in my projects even when I lacked it myself. She was the first to whet my appetite for Noritake wares made in the 1921-41 era. She encouraged me to write the first Noritake book as well as the three Nippon books. I could always count on her help and guidance. She is missed. She was loved.

# About the Author

Joan Van Patten is the author of four other books published by Collector Books, *The Collector's Encyclopedia of Nippon Porcelain*, *The Collector's Encyclopedia of Nippon Porcelain, Series II*, *The Collector's Encyclopedia of Nippon Porcelain, Series III*, and *The Collector's Encyclopedia of Noritake*. She has also compiled numerous price guides covering the items found in these books.

She has authored two booklets entitled *The Nippon Primer* and *The Nippon SPOTTER*. She has also written numerous trade paper and magazine articles which have been featured in *The Antique Trader Weekly*, *The Antique Trader Price Guide*, *The Antique Trader Yearly*, *Schroeder's Insider*, *American Collector*, *National Journal*, *Orientalia Journal*, *N.E. Country Antiques*, *Antiques and Collector's Mart*, *Spinning Wheel*, the *INCC Newsletter*, the *Nippon Notebook*, *Noritake News*, and others.

She was the co-founder of the INCC (International Nippon Collectors' Club) and served as its first president. She has lectured on the subject of Nippon and Noritake at numerous antique shows and seminars. Research and travel are other major interests of the author.

# Acknowledgments

As Montaigne once wrote "I have gathered a bouquet of other men's flowers,
and only the ribbon that binds them is my own."

In this book, I too have only supplied the ribbon to the bouquet of knowledge and photos found within it. This book exists due to the result of many collectors' information, expertise, and photos. Thanks to all who helped and special thanks to the following people:

Bill Schroeder and Collector Books who continue to have faith in my projects. This company is number one to work with!

My friend, Viola Breves, sent me many photos but most of all she helped with the price guide which is a huge task now that there are over 1400 items shown between the two books. Vi is a longtime collector of Noritake and very knowledgeable in the field. She has helped with both books and subsequent price guides and her expertise has been invaluable.

David Spain sent me two chapters for the book, many photos, and found other collectors who were willing to send in photos. David did an incredible amount of research for this book and I am very appreciative of his efforts. He also edits the *Noritake News* which is a must for collectors. This is a very informative newsletter and subscription information may be obtained by writing directly to him at 1237 Federal Ave. E, Seattle, WA 98102.

My friends, Earl Smith and Mark Griffin, have a fantastic collection and some of their super pieces are found both in the book and on the cover. They selected Clement Photographic Services, Inc. from Fort Myers, FL and I am very pleased with the finished product. They also gave me their support and encouragement throughout this whole project for which I am grateful.

Sheldon and Sayo Harmeling sent me over 300 photos! Two boxes arrived from them and just as I would ooh and aah over one picture, the next one would be even better. Getting descriptions on this many items is a mon-umental task. How do you adequately thank people like this? Words are not enough.

Margaret Anderson sent me nearly 100 photos of her items and information for one of my chapters. She had some wonderful pieces to share and her photography skills are oustanding. Thank you, Margaret.

My thanks and gratitude also go to Polly Frye who wrote the chapter on photographing your collection. Polly is a professional photographer and her information should be of help to all collectors. Dennis Burnickas sent me several photos and his chapter "A Dealer's Viewpoint" should be of interest to both collectors and dealers.

Others who contributed 40 or more photos are Deidre Cimiano, William and Lauren Higgins, Marilyn, Ted, and Mike Gendelman, Norm Derrin, Marilyn Derrin, Tim Trapani, Kimberly Carman, and Mary Lou Gross. Thank you so much for your help with the book.

Others who helped with photos and/or information are Doug Funnell, Diane Wohlever, Judy Boyd, Kathy Wojciechowski, Bernie Golden, Nelda and David Newburn, Jess Berry, Susan Corwin, Wendy Van Patten, Marie Young, Michael Owen, Bob and Bernadette Jackson, and Wendy Noritake.

I know that a few people are going to be disappointed to find that some of their photos were not used in this book but many were duplicates of another collector's pieces and I tried to select the best photos available. However, I do think that all who helped with this project will be excited to be able to view nearly 1000 more new and wonderful pieces which are featured in this second book.

Thanks to all who helped make this book a reality!

# Table of Contents

# Introduction

Just as a caterpillar turns into a beautiful butterfly, Noritake items (circa 1921-41) are also going through a transformation period. These pieces were once reasonably priced and abundantly found. Not so today. They were a collectible without "status" but that too has changed. All of a sudden it seems that everyone is taking a new look at these old castaways.

Although these items were manufactured in Japan, they were intended for export to the United States. In fact, according to company sources most of the designs were drawn in the United States and then sent to the company headquarters in Japan for the artists to copy. Hence, American designs were made available on the less expensive Japanese porcelain wares. This was an opportunity for the middle class in the United States to enjoy fine porcelain at a reasonable price.

Noritake wares from the 1921-41 period were high quality, low priced items. They were made available to the American public in department stores, gift shops and through mail order catalogs. Mass-production techniques were used via assembly lines. After the outbreak of World War I in Europe, industrialization in Japan picked up at a greater pace. The European factories had turned to the manufacture of items for war production and this proved to be an economic opportunity for Japan enabling her to increase sales in already established markets and also new areas.

The 1911 Factory Law in Japan (which incidentally was not enforced until 1916) prescribed a maximum of an 11 hour work day for women and children and a minimum working age of 12. The 1926 amendment shortened the hours to ten and increased the minimum age to 14. This provided a large work force and certainly could account for the great amount of Japanese items that reached our shores during this period.

Nagoya, Japan is the location of the Noritake Company in Japan. Nagoya is located in the very heart of Central Japan, one of the nation's key industrial zones. Historically, Nagoya was a typical castle town of feudal Japan, growing up around a number of castles built in the 16th century. It is located approximately ten miles from the small village of Seto. Seto is known for its large deposits of kaolin and it's been estimated that there is enough clay there to last at least another hundred years.

Collecting Noritake wares is not only enjoyable but also educational. As we study the designs and scenes portrayed we learn more about our past. There's a nostalgia boom going on, a yearning for the good old days. Most collectors want to find out an item's history, how old it is, how it was made, and its value.

Alice Morse Earle wrote a book in 1892 entitled *China Collecting in America*. A quote that I like seems just as applicable today as then. "What fancies we weave, what dreams we dream over a piece of homely old china! Every cup, every jar in our china ingatherings, has the charm of fantasy, visions of past life and beauty though only imagined. I like to think that the china I love has been warmly loved before, has been made a cherished companion, been tenderly handled ere I took it to be my companion and to care for it. It is much the same friendly affection that I feel for an old well-read, half-worn book; the unknown hands through which it has passed, the unseen eyes that have gazed on it, have endeared it to me. This imagined charm exists in china if it be old, though we know not a word of its past, save that it has a past and is not fresh from the potter's wheel and the kiln. The very haze of uncertainty is favorable to the fancies of a dreamer; I summon past owners from that shadowy hiding-place; weave romances out of that cloud; build past dwelling-houses more quaint, more romantic than any in whose windows I have gazed, whose threshold I have trodden in my real china-hunting."

Noritake collecting trends have also changed over the years. Most collectors are no longer purchasing individual cups and saucers and cute little relish dishes and they don't want damaged items! They have become much more sophisticated and cautious in their buying and most have discovered that the really well-executed pieces in MINT condition always hold their value. When articles are cracked, chipped, repaired, have extensive worn gold, not complete such as a humidor lacking a cover, then adjustments must be reflected in their price. A $500 humidor in mint condition may be worth only $50 without its lid and then one must search diligently for a buyer. Collectors should try to steer away from these types of items unless they are purchased very reasonably and/or bought merely for decorating purposes. They are not a good investment.

Collecting fads will also push up prices temporarily. What's hot today may not be a year from now and prices could drop dramatically. Rare items become rarer with the passage of time and as the world population increases and more people grow interested in a collectible there is a greater demand but diminished supply. Well-executed rare pieces in mint condition will always be desired and hold their value.

In the last few years Art Deco style pieces have captured the fancy of Noritake collectors and the prices are skyrocketing because of their popularity. In case you haven't noticed it always pays to start collecting an item BEFORE it's stylish to do so. I heard a collector lamenting lately that he wished he'd bought a hundred Noritake powder puff boxes decorated with Art Deco style ladies for he would now be able to sell them and buy the little cottage by the ocean he so desires.

The Art Deco designs we find on our Noritake wares are associated with the Roaring Twenties period. The change in the designs records the social changes of this time span. This was a period of gay abandon and hectic frivolity, totally different than the stuffy Victorian era that preceded it. Many of these pieces show the fashion trends and life styles of the period. We find cloche-capped flappers (the flapper had just emerged as the newly liberated woman),

upswept skirts, wide brimmed hats, raised hemlines, turbans adorned with feathers, top-hatted gentlemen wearing capes, décolleté gowns, streamlined dogs such as the greyhound or borzois, and costumed ladies. We have clowns playing mandolins, gay Parisian cocottes with bobbed hair and long dangling earrings. There are tango dancer scenes portraying the night life of the period.

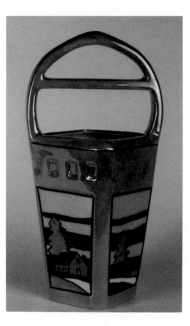

*Above: Powder puff box, $250.00; Left: Vase, 6½" high.*

*Clockwise starting with top left photo: Lemon dish, 5¼" wide; Tray, 10¾" x 8½"; Vase, 6¼" tall, $30.00; Smoking tray, 8½" long; Plate, 8½" wide, $250.00.*

Many of the Art Deco designs found are imitative of pre-Columbian art and the architecture of Mexico and Central America. Some resemble the Aztec style of decoration. We also find other designs that are copies of southwest American Indian articles – the stylized birds, flowers, deer, sun, and cloud patterns and lightning motifs.

Research indicates that the 1922 opening of King Tutankhamen's tomb in Egypt helped to make Egyptian decorative ideas a popular theme during this time period. The Ballets Russes under the direction of Sergei Deaghilev also influenced some of the designs. The term "Art Deco" is an Anglicized term and was not used until the mid-1960s. It had its start at the Exposition Internationale des Arts Décoratifs et Industriels Modernes in Paris in 1925.

My advice to the novice collector is to study and study some more. He should visit shops, shows and auctions, read all the books and information he can on the subject and talk with both dealers and collectors about Nippon pieces. He should also familiarize himself with Nippon era wares (circa 1891-1921). These immediately preceded the 1921-41 Noritake period covered in this book. Some of the items are similar in shape as well as decoration. Most of these pieces were produced by the Noritake Company and it's a good idea to make comparisons between the two. Today's collector should ask questions and handle the pieces whenever possible. Beginners should make modest purchases initially but they also should have the courage to try out their OWN taste even if a mistake or two is made.

*(Above and below) A large variety of
Noritake pieces found at a recent auction.*

When determining the value and price of a piece, collectors should consider the workmanship and the condition first, then its rarity and its present popularity. Will the piece enhance the rest of the collection? If, after considering all these points the buyer still genuinely likes the piece and can afford it, I think he should buy it. For no matter what the erratic and constantly changing market does he will have a collectible he can personally enjoy each day.

It is my hope that in this "Second Series" on Noritake porcelain, collectors will learn new information and get the opportunity to see more new and wonderful pieces of Noritake wares. In a short time you can obtain information that took me and others many years to gain. J.D. Salinger once wrote "What really knocks me out is a book that, when you're all done reading it, you wish the author that wrote it was a terrific friend of yours and you could call him up on the phone whenever you felt like it." Hopefully, this book will leave you with that same feeling.

# Bits of Yesterday

It's always exciting to go through old catalogs and spot some of the same Noritake pieces one has in the china cabinet. And then a glance at the original price compared to today's – well, it can be quite a shock.

In 1928 individual butter dishes sold for 45¢ a dozen. A figural lady dresser doll for $2.00 and a figural lady talcum powder shaker for $2.00. Other prices in the twenties:

Toothpick holder, 50¢

Bonbon dish, $1.40 – some even sold for $2.00–3.75 a dozen

Honey jar with figural bumble bees, $3.00

Tea set, $5.00

Wall vase, $2.00

Pair of napkin rings, $2.00

Novelty items – figural ashtrays and salt and pepper shakers, $9.60 a gross

*The Dutch girl and swan salt and pepper shaker set sold in 1928 for $1.50. The house-shaped salt and pepper set sold for 6¢ a set back in the twenties.*

*The salt and pepper shakers in this condiment set sold for 6–9¢ each.*

Toy china tea sets were advertised for $1.00–2.25. Some came with six tea plates, cups, saucers, one covered teapot, one covered sugar bowl and one cream pitcher. Old ads show that some sets however, were sold with only three or four plates, cups and saucers. If an odd number of plates or cups is found today in a set we often think there are parts missing or broken and we may be wrong. Now we know that may not be the case.

Teapots were often sold with matching tea tiles. The items were also sold separately.

Through the Butler Bros. catalogs, stores could buy a 60-piece assortment for $39.00 or approximately 65¢ each. That assortment included marmalade jars, flower arrangers, vases, cigarette boxes, wall pockets, spooners, etc.

When today's collector sees that a more commonly found sandwich tray sold for about $1.00 back then while some of the figural ashtrays sold for as little as 6¢ each, it's hard to believe the disparity between the two today. Figural ashtrays often sell for hundreds of dollars while most sandwich trays bring a price under $100.00.

*Two figural ashtrays. Similar ones sold for 6–8¢ each in the twenties. Wouldn't we love to find bargains like that today!*

# Colorful Imported China
## Lovely Gifts — Beautifully Boxed

Vanity Set No. 93
$3.50 with PREMIUM

Ash Tray No. 75
$1 with PREM.

Seasoning Set No. 96
$3 with PREMIUM

Salt Dip Set No. 80
$1.50 with PREMIUM

Dresser Doll No. 91 $2 with PREMIUM

Talcum Powder Shaker No. 81
$2 with PREMIUM

Salt and Pepper Set No. 146 $1 with PREMIUM

Wall Vase No. 88
$2 with PREMIUM

Cake Plate No. 143
$3 with PREM.

Perfume Bottle No. 142
$1.50 with PREMIUM

Sugar and Cream Set No. 151 90c with PREMIUM

Relish Dish No. 78
$1.50 with PREMIUM

Condiment Set No. 83
$2.50 with PREMIUM

Toothpick Holder No. 149 50c with PREM.

Napkin Rings No. 148
$1 with PREMIUM

Berry Sugar and Cream Set No. 144
$2.50 with PREMIUM

Mayonnaise Set No. 84
$3 with PREMIUM

Bon Bon Dish No. 76
$1.40 with PREMIUM

Honey Jar No. 145
$3 with PREMIUM

Bon Bon Dish No. 77
$2.25 with PREMIUM

Sugar and Cream Set No. 92
$2.50 with PREM.

Refreshment Set No. 86
$3.75 with PREMIUM

Salt and Pepper Set No. 79 $1.50 with PREMIUM

Salt and Pepper Set No. 147
60c with PREMIUM

Vase No. 150
$2 with PREMIUM

Sugar and Cream Set No. 82
$2.50 with PREMIUM

11

## POWDER JARS

Y2904 Y2900 Y2902

"Colonial Belle" figures, fine quality light weight china, matte and iridescent finishes, dainty pastel tinted dresses with contrasting trims, tinted faces and hair.

**Y2904**—2¼ in. Asstd. 2 doz. in carton. **Doz 82c**

**Y2900**—3 in. Asstd. **6 styles.** 1 doz. in carton.................... **Doz $1.95**

**Y2902**—6½ in. Asstd. **3 styles.** ¼ doz. in carton.................... **Doz $7.75**

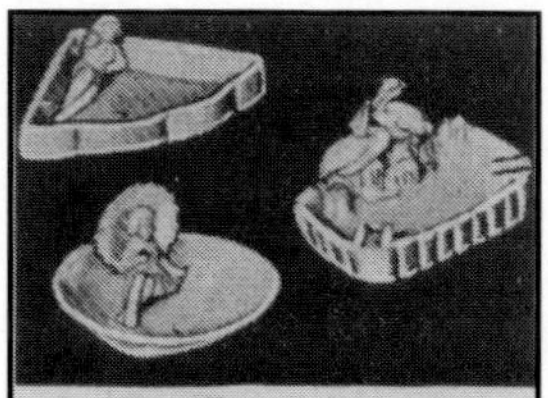

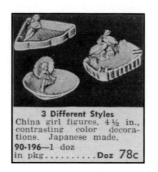

**3 Different Styles**

China girl figures, 4½ in., contrasting color decorations. Japanese made.

**90-196**—1 doz in pkg.......... **Doz 78c**

## China Wall Pocket No. 3

**$2** *with Premium*

Handsomely painted in scenic effect on a background of blue luster. A decidedly smart means of displaying decorative flowers. Hole in back for hanging. Height, 8¼ in. Mlg. wt. 1½ lbs.

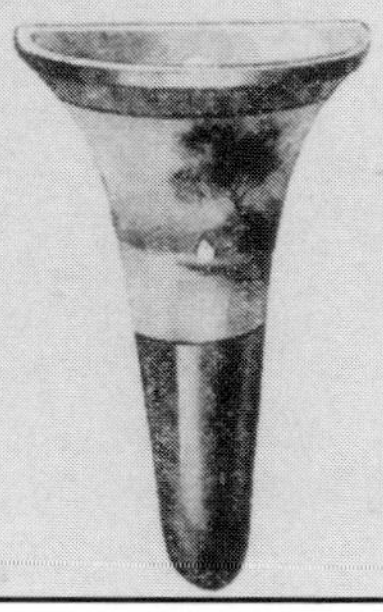

## HAND PAINTED JAPANESE CHINA

Pure white high grade Japanese trademarked china, harmonizing tinted allover rural pictures in pastel shades, gold striped edges and handles.

**R8901—Bread and butter plates,** 6 in. diam., coupe shape. 1 doz. in pkg. **Doz $2.00**

**R8902—Pie or tea plates,** 7⅝ in. diam., **6 decorations.** ½ doz. in pkg. **Doz $3.95**

## SALAD BOWL

**R2801 — 3 decorations,** 8¾ in., china, fancy deep paneled shape, blue, pink and green lusters, shadow flower and gold scroll medallions, large tinted rose. Asstd. ½ doz. in pkg.......... **Doz $3.95**

## 7-PC. BERRY SET

**R3386**—China, deep, pink rose bouquet center, deep ivory tints with black outlined tangerine panels, dish 9¼ in., 6 nappies, 5¼ in. 1 set in pkg. **SET (7 pcs) $1.35**

## SALTS AND PEPPERS

**R6755—6 styles,** luster china, asstd. flower and bird designs, fancy shape, natural tints, cork bottom, asstd. 12 in box. 4 doz. (4 boxes) in pkg.......... **Doz 72c**

**R6826**—2 in. blue luster birds, terra cotta bills, black eyes. ½ doz. in box..... **Doz 96c**

**R5053**—Lt. wt. white china, Japanese red landscape decoration, red edges and handle, cup 3¾x2, saucer 5⅜ in. 2 doz. in pkg. **DOZ (24 pcs) $1.40**
30 doz. or more, **Doz 1.27**

**R1204M**—Lt. wt. Japanese china, luster border with gold rim, bright floral spray, cup 3⅞x2, saucer 5½ in. 2 doz. in pkg. **DOZ (24 pcs) $1.89**

## BISQUE FLOWER BLOCKS

**R8040—6 styles,** 3 in., bisque, perforated, highly glazed, ivory effect bodies, graceful girl figures in different poses. Asstd. 1 doz. in pkg........ **Doz 82c**

## BONBON DISHES

**E-7042**—½ doz. in pkg. **Doz $2.00**

7½ in., light weight Japanese china, 2-tone luster effect, blue and green bands, landscape and floral decorations, gold handles.

**E-7041**—¼ doz. in pkg. **Doz $3.75**

**2 styles,** 7¼ in., deep octagon shape, light weight Japanese china, **3 decorations,** asstd. blue, green and red, bright colorful flower decorations, black edges, green decorated detachable bamboo handle.

## CUPS AND SAUCERS
### Ovide Shape

**R40900** — Translucent white china, allover "Howo Bird" and scroll decorations in 2 tints of oriental blue, cup 3¾x2, saucer 5½ in. 2 doz. in pkg. DOZ (24 pcs) **$1.20**
30 doz. or more, Doz **1.12**

**R1204M** — Lt. wt. Japanese china, luster border with gold rim, bright floral spray, cup 3⅞x2, saucer 5½ in. 2 doz. in pkg. DOZ (24 pcs) **$1.75**

**R5050** — Light wt. white china, cup 3¾x2, saucer 5½ in. 2 doz. in pkg. DOZ (24 pcs) **$1.20**
30 doz. or more, Doz **1.08**

**R6813** — Light weight china, allover blue luster, tan luster inside cup, solid blue handles. Cup 3⅞x2, saucer 5½ in. 1 doz. in pkg. DOZ (24 pcs) **$2.10**

---

## BIG VOLUME SELLERS
### Priced About 10% Less Than Domestic

The staple, universally known, Japanese china cups and saucers—ovide shapes, pure white, light weight china, both plain and with gold band. Good quality and good packing.

**R5050** — Cup 3¾x2, saucer 5½ in., plain white light weight china. 2 doz. in pkg. DOZ (24 pcs) **$1.35**

**R5073** — Cup 3¾x2, saucer 5½ in.; wide gold edge and striped handle. 2 doz. in pkg. DOZ (24 pcs) **$1.68**

---

## F. O. B. Baltimore
### Famous "HOWO BIRD" Asst.

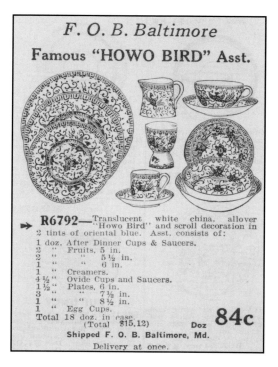

**R6792** — Translucent white china, allover "Howo Bird" and scroll decoration in 2 tints of oriental blue. Asst. consists of:

1 doz. After Dinner Cups & Saucers.
2 " Fruits, 5 in.
2 " " 5½ in.
1 " " 6 in.
1 " Creamers.
4½ " Ovide Cups and Saucers.
1½ " Plates, 6 in.
3 " " 7½ in.
1 " " 8½ in.
1 " Egg Cups.
Total 18 doz. in case.
(Total $15.12)

Doz **84c**

Shipped F. O. B. Baltimore, Md.
Delivery at once.

---

## TOY CHINA TEA SET

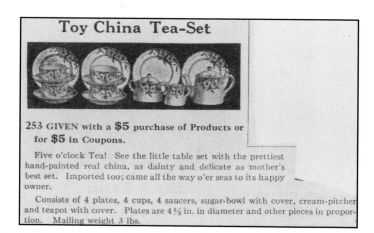

23-pc. Tea Set of lustrous imported Japanese china. 6 cups, 6 saucers, 6 plates, covered teapot, cream pitcher, covered sugar bowl. Attractively decorated in tan; floral designs in bright colors. Plates, 3¾ in. in diameter; other pieces in proportion. Mlg. wt. 2½ lbs. **2322** *Given for $1 in Coupons*

---

## Toy China Tea Set No. 152

No. 7 for adoption. Made enmposition arms and eyes and g over all. white or titched in 8 oz.

0c ith EM.

A complete service for six! Fine Japanese Lustre China. Delightfully decorated with Dutch scene painted on white background with tan lustre border. Set consists of six tea plates, six cups, six saucers, one covered tea-pot, one covered sugar bowl and one cream pitcher. Tea plates are 3¾ in. in diameter, other pieces in proportion. Mlg. wt. 2 lbs.

**$2** *with PREM.*

---

## Toy China Tea-Set

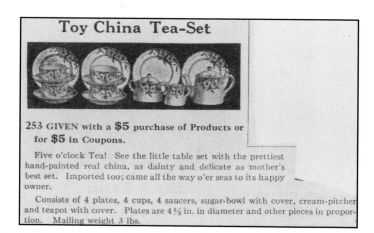

**253 GIVEN** with a **$5** purchase of Products or for **$5** in Coupons.

Five o'clock Tea! See the little table set with the prettiest hand-painted real china, as dainty and delicate as mother's best set. Imported too; came all the way o'er seas to its happy owner.

Consists of 4 plates, 4 cups, 4 saucers, sugar-bowl with cover, cream-pitcher and teapot with cover. Plates are 4⅜ in. in diameter and other pieces in proportion. Mailing weight 3 lbs.

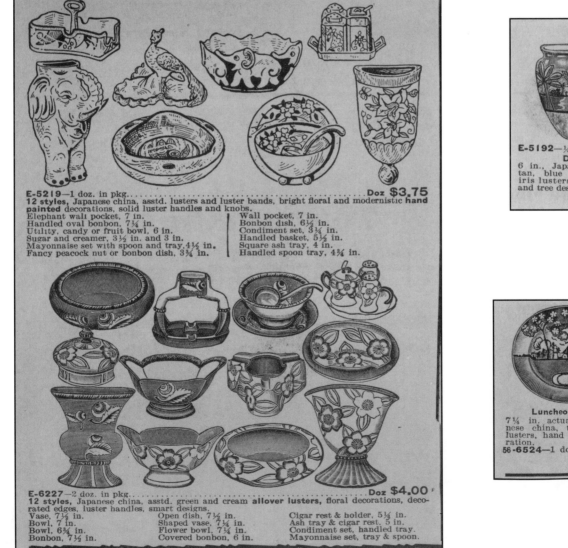

14

# IMPORTED CHINA (Continued)

R3710 R3711

### Egg Cups

**R3710**—1⅞x2¼, pure white. 1 doz. in pkg......**Doz 37c**

**R3711**—1⅞x2⅜, gold band. 1 doz. in pkg......**Doz 39c**

### Condiment Set

**R6203**—4 pcs., tan luster with metallic blue bands and enameled floral sprays, gold tops and handles, 4¼ in. compartment tray, salt & pepper and mustard pot with spoon. ½ doz. sets in pkg....**Doz sets $3.75**

### Salt and Pepper Shakers

**R6749** — Individuals, asstd. allover brown, iris and blue lusters, colored bills, black eyes, cork bottoms, asstd. 6 in box. 1 doz. (2 boxes) in pkg..............**Doz 75c**

### Salt and Pepper Shakers

**R5311**—China, 2-tone blue and tan luster, bird in relief, each set in gift box. ½ doz. sets in pkg. **Doz sets $3.95**

### Two Tone Luster 7 Pc. Berry Set

**R3312**—Imported china, **2-tone luster,** amber center, wide blue band, black hairline, dish 9 in., SIX individuals 5 in. 1 set in pkg. **SET (7 pcs) $1.20**

### Sugar and Creamer Set

**R3219**—Creamer 3⅛ in., sugar 3¾ in., fine china, squat paneled shape, allover amber luster, white stenciled daisy spray, black edges, handles and knobs. ¼ doz. sets in pkg. **Doz sets $6.25**

### Japanese China Plates

Allover Japanese landscape scene in colors, red edge. 1 doz. in pkg.

**R9530**—6⅛ in..**Doz $0.89**

**R9538**—7¼ " . " **1.20**

### 7 Pc. Berry Set

**R3390**—China, deep, rose bouquet center, blue luster panel border, gold medallions, scattered inner rose sprays. Dish 8⅝ in., 6 nappies 4⅞ in. 1 set in pkg. **SET (7 pcs) 90c**

**R2807**—3 decorations, 9¼ in., china, deep shape, all over shaded tan luster, large vari-color floral sprays, blue, green and bronze scroll decorations. Asstd. ½ doz. in pkg. **Doz $4.00**

### 13 Piece Chocolate Sets

**R6480**—China, Japanese scene in colors, Tokio red fancy handle and knob, pot 9¼ in., 6 cups and 6 saucers. 1 set in pkg. **SET (13 pcs) $1.50**

## Toy China Tea Set

**2747 With $2.25** *Purchase or Coupons*

Lovely set imported from Japan. Set consists of teapot, sugar bowl with cover, cream pitcher, 4 cups, 4 saucers and 4 plates. Decorated with blue luster band and red flowers. Plates are 3½ in. in diameter; other pieces in proportion. **Postage 6c.**

## Luster China Ash Trays

**E-6944**—Diamond shape
**E-6945**—Heart shape.
**E-6946**—Spade shape
**E-6947**—Club shape. **Doz 85c**
1 doz. in pkg.

Average 3¾x3½ in., Japanese china, asstd. allover lusters, 2 cut-out cigarette rests, figure in relief, black line edge.

## Toy China Tea Set No. 90

Imported Japanese Toy China Tea Set with which the youngster can make merry playing tea-party. Set consists of three cups, three saucers, teapot with cover, sugar bowl with cover and cream pitcher. Decorated with a bright blue band and gaily colored birds and flowers on a white background. Teapot, 3½ in. high; other pieces in proportion. Mailing weight 2 lbs.

**$1** *with PREMIUM*

## CELERY TRAYS



**E-7075**—¼ doz. in pkg. **Doz $3.95**

10½x5¼ in., light weight Japanese china, solid blue, bright yellow and coral hand painted floral decorations black edges, open handles.

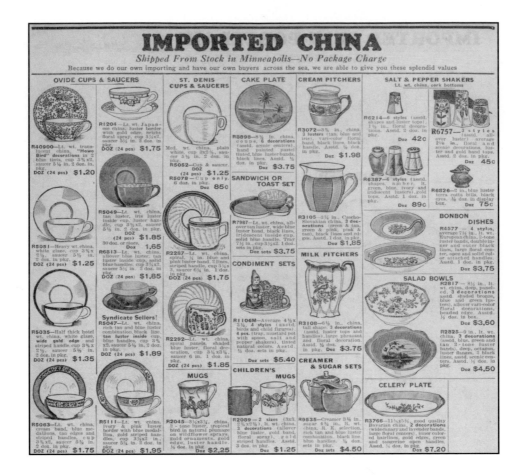

Once I decided to do a second Noritake book, I knew right away that I wanted to include in it the lighthearted but thought-provoking essay that appears below. The original version first appeared in the March 1990 issue of *Noritake News* (Volume II, #1). The version below was prepared especially for this book and appears here with permission of *Noritake News*.

JVP

# Noritake: A Closer Look
## by: David H. Spain

When you are in an antique store or hiking around a large show and you happen to find a piece of Noritake that you think you might like to buy, what is one of the very first things you do? Well, if you are like most collectors I know, you probably will examine the piece very carefully, looking for hairline cracks, paint flecks, and other "conditional details." Usually, it is only if it passes this scrutiny that one begins to "talk turkey" with the dealer.

Although this is indisputably sound practice, I believe this initial scrutiny is too often the last time we take such a close look at our pieces and this is unfortunate because Noritake porcelains warrant repeated close examination, not because we may have missed a flaw or because our pieces might have developed cracks while sitting on our display shelves. Rather, I want to explore the claim – my claim – that one's enjoyment of a collection of porcelains as beautiful as those we collect can be greatly enhanced if we will but take the time to give the pieces in our collection a closer look.

In order to enhance the odds that you will really enjoy this essay, I must ask you to take the trouble – not now as you read these words, but in just a few moments from now – to do two things: (1) get up out of your comfortable chair to retrieve your copy of Joan Van Patten's *The Collector's Encyclopedia of Noritake First Series* and (2) position yourself near some of your best pieces of Noritake. I do hope you'll agree to do it; otherwise, much of what I have to say will be rather abstract or, perhaps I should say, so much more *distant* than it should be. So you won't miss anything, I plan to pause for a few minutes while you take care of these essential tasks. You should start thinking about getting ready to get up out of your chair because the moment for action is just about

here. The time to get your Noritake "bible" and to seat yourself right next to your best Noritake is NOW.

Turn to page 109 of your Van Patten book and take a look at the shallow bowl on the right in plate 30. Beautiful, isn't it? And fairly small, too – only 6.5" in diameter, exclusive of its rather "Nipponish" handles. To illustrate the point I am wanting to make, we can start with this bowl. You don't have it, you say? It doesn't matter, for a portion of it appears below.

In the photograph here, the bird is larger than it is

on the bowl. A straight line from the beak to the lower back part of the head is, on the bowl, about .75"; in the photo it is well over an inch. This fact – i.e., the fact that it is larger than in real life – helps one to take a closer look. But there is more at work here than this. Only a portion of the bird appears in the picture. This also (and obviously) forces you to take a closer look. And, when one does so, the effects can be quite strong as well as pleasant. Look at the colors on the bird's chest and at the tips of the wing feathers. Notice its eye: it seems to be looking up – perhaps at you. Do you routinely notice such details when looking at the piece as a whole? I don't; indeed, I can't.

Now I want you to try something, even though it may seem a little weird. Bring the close-up photo of the bird up toward your eyes so that it is as close as it can get and still be in focus. Now stare at it for 10 to 20 seconds. Do you find yourself falling into the world of that bird just a little bit? No? Does it sound too silly? People will vary on this, of course. But when that photo of the bird is just a few inches from my eyes, thus cutting off all other visual sensations in the room, I find it hard to think of anything but that bird. And I enjoy that. It doesn't require hours or minutes, mind you (the 1960's are long gone, after all); just a few seconds will do the trick.

Unconvinced? Puzzled? Intrigued? Well whatever, let's try another one. Turn to page 110 of your Van Patten and look at plate 34. I don't have that exact item in my collection, but I have one that is very similar. In size and shape, it is like the bowl in plate 23 (p.108). The painting differs in mine from the one shown in plate 34 because the lady on my bowl is holding some flowers and her head is turned to the right. Even so, the design shown on the piece in the Van Patten book (Volume I) will give you an idea of what the whole piece looks like.

Now look at the photo above. What appears in the photo as 2" is just over an inch on my bowl. So what we see obviously is larger but, as I've said, it also is just a portion of the whole. Does the feeling change when you shift your gaze back and forth between the whole and the part? It does for me. Put the photo in this book as close as you can to the photo of the piece in Volume One, and shift your gaze back and forth. What happens? What

thoughts come to you? Again, they must vary a great deal from one person to the next (and, for many of you by this time, your thoughts probably are questions about whether or not I am sane). Be that as it may, I find my thoughts focusing on the position of the woman's left shoulder. She is shy, isn't she? Now try bringing the close-up photo closer to your eyes. Can you, to use a phrase, "get in touch" with her shyness?

Let's try this again with Van Patten plate 80 on page 117. A significantly enlarged portion (her head, hair and all, is .75" wide on the tile; in the photo, it is over 1.5") appears below. With the closely cropped enlargement, I tend to see her, simply, as dreamily sniffing the flower. The photograph of the whole, however, tends to pull my

eyes toward her dress and I get the feeling that she is in an arrogant mood. Thus, our whole sense of a piece may change as a function of how closely we look at it.

By now, there should be no need to belabor the subject since surely you have got the idea. So, I will discuss the other photos more briefly. Turn to page 131 of your book (Volume One) and have a look at plate 164. A very much enlarged portion of it appears on the top of page 20. From the left edge of the flower to the tip of the hat brim is, on the plaque itself, about 1.75" while in the photo above it is almost 5". What did her friend do to justify such a look, anyway? Or, are her eyes and lips expressing ambivalence or uncertainty? What do you think?

Lastly, turn to page 132 and plate 170. Portions of the left and center pieces are shown in the photos on the next page. You'll have no trouble identifying which is

*Close-up of plate #170, middle item.*

*Close-up of plate #170, first item.*

which. The doll in the photo is over two-and-a-half times the size of the doll on the plaque itself. It seems she almost has a smirk on her face, doesn't it? Or is it just my imagination.

Of course it is. That is my point, at least in part. If we use our imaginations a bit, we can get more enjoyment out of the pieces in our collections. And one way to foster such imaginative moments is to take a closer look at what we have worked so hard to find. And, as for the many possibilities, that too is one point I am trying to make. Most of the time, there is no obvious right or wrong; the possibilities, if not endless, are certainly numerous. One can ask many questions of the pieces in one's collection – if you get close enough. This is not to deny that there are advantages and insights that come

from looking at the whole from some distance. It is, rather, merely a suggestion that we stop, from time to time, to take a closer look.

Now, if you played along with me at the start of this essay, then you should be seated relatively close to some of your best Noritake. That being the case, I would suggest that now might be a good time to try giving some of your own Noritake a closer look. Go on. Try it. Take a few minutes *now* to have a really close look at some of your favorite pieces. You might see something you never saw before. Besides, I have been assured by the author of the next chapter that he will wait for you as long as need be. So enjoy your efforts, and those of the many designers and artists who produced the pieces you have so lovingly accumulated. You – and they – deserve it.

*This is an enlargement of plate 164 that is seen in its entirety in Noritake First Series, as discussed on page 18.*

*The doll is over two-and-a-half times the size of the doll on the plaque itself. It seems she almost has a smirk on her face, doesn't it? Or is it just my imagination?*

*In addition to his family and professional life (he is a member of the cultural anthropology faculty at the University of Washington), David Spain edits Noritake News the newsletter for collectors of and dealers in Noritake lusterware and other Noritake collectibles (excluding dinnerware). He is aided in this endeavor by his good friend and former anthropology department colleague Michael G. Owen, publisher. Readers interested in subscription information may write to the editor at 1237 Federal Avenue East, Seattle, WA 98102.*

I heard David Spain give a lecture on Art Deco Noritake at a meeting of the International Nippon Collectors' Club and I asked him if he would write up a version of his talk for it. The essay that follows is much more than and rather different from that talk. Even so, it is informally written and, I hope you will agree, offers much for us to think about.

JVP

# Searching for Art Deco Noritake and the Elements of a Style: A Personal Account
## by: David H. Spain

### Introduction

"I don't know much about art, but I know what I like." That clichéd phrase, which is offered all too often in a tone of dry contempt by art experts as they presume to characterize the views of collectors who they think are either uniformed or merely opinionated, could have been applied quite validly to me, especially in the early days of my search for great Noritake lusterware. I knew I liked "Art Deco" pieces and, for various reasons, I was fairly confident of my ability to recognize the style when scanning the diverse array of stuff one finds on the typical display table at shows. I also knew, however, that I could say very little about the style's history or characteristic features and I could not usefully articulate to anyone what the grounds were for granting a given piece of Noritake the coveted title "Deco."

Instead, collecting Art Deco Noritake was, for me, a lot like swimming or riding a bicycle: it is a lot easier to do than to talk about. This, I think, is the more friendly point of the clichéd phrase with which I opened this essay. It acknowledges that there is a difference between "knowing" and "knowing about" something. If, to take another example, you have a toothache you *know* cavities; it takes a dentist, however, to know *about* cavities. Similarly, many collectors know Art Deco Noritake when they see it; indeed, they'll knock down good friends to get to it first. It takes a specialist, however, (e.g., an art historian) to know about this style.

It should be emphasized, therefore, that I am not an art historian. Rather, and as will become steadily more apparent, especially to those readers who are art historians, I am a collector. As such, my primary aim is and has always been quite simple: to find Art Deco Noritake. Eventually, however, I began to feel I should look not just for more pieces but also for better information about the elements of Art Deco as a style. In this essay, I share with you some of the results of that effort. In doing so, I discuss not only what I think the elements of the style are but also how I came to learn what I did about it.

Although I am confident some of the Noritake collectors who read this will find portions of what I say informative and, I hope at least thought-provoking if not controversial, I would emphasize that this is not a learned treatise on "Deco" as an art style. This is so because, quite simply, I have neither the credentials nor the time and space necessary to present an authoritative account. Those wishing to read more definitive and expert discussions should consult one or more of the many fine books on Art Deco that one can find in any good public library (some examples are described at the end of this chapter). In contrast to those books, this essay is a more personal account of my explorations into this complex and often murky territory. Alert readers will, therefore, want to take what I say here with the requisite grains of salt.

Although my knowledge of the style steadily grew, especially regarding materials produced by the Noritake Company in its line of luster "fancy wares," it still is not incorrect to say that, for nearly 10 years, I was a walking case of my opening remark. That is, I knew what I liked but had almost no idea what it was that really made a piece "leap out" and say, in effect, "you must buy me!" That does not mean, however, that I sat on my duff, paralyzed by a lack of formal knowledge. No indeed; I was, during those years, actively looking and buying – so much so that, in about 10 years, I had quite a few nice pieces of Art Deco Noritake and a few outstanding ones.

I must also note, however, that I bought scores of pieces that I would later (sometimes the next day) regret owning. What is worse, I also must confess that I passed up some real gems that I still don't like being reminded

21

of. All in all, however, I am convinced by my experiences that it is possible to put together a reasonable collection while working "instinctively" or, more properly, intuitively. Although some experts will disagree, I do not think it is essential that one be able to cite chapter and verse from expert sources in order to make good purchase decisions.

Indeed, I rather enjoyed using a more-or-less intuitive approach in my hunt for Art Deco Noritake. Even so, I neither relied entirely on intuition nor would I recommend that anyone do so. I enjoyed the kick I got from the really quite visceral experience of seeing a piece that was totally new to me and feeling, instantly and often with quite a jolt, that (a) I "had to have it" and (b) that I surely was looking at a piece in the Art Deco style even though I could not explain what it was, precisely, that enabled me to know it. But I wouldn't recommend it to anyone as the sole method, however (and even with all the visceral excitement) because, as I have said, I made many mistakes – far more than I would have had I known then what I know now, consciously, about the style.

I was exposed, eventually, to expert opinions about Art Deco as a style. Mostly and at first, however, my ideas developed in the course of the many long and interesting conversations I had with collector friends who, for the most part, were as much in the dark as I was. Although these discussions definitely were helpful, the best *potential* source of information I ever had was in the person of Howard Kottler. Sadly, I am forced to stress the word "potential" because, before I or virtually anyone could really tap this source to its depths, he was taken from me, and from all of us, by an untimely death in January 1989.

Howard was a remarkable man in many, many ways. I did not know of him until late in 1983. At that time, I found out about what had been described to me as "his book" called *Noritake Art Deco Porcelains*. When I learned of it, I made a bee-line for the best bookstore in Seattle only to discover, after considerable effort, that they did not carry it and that this "book" was in fact a small but invaluable catalog published at the start of a traveling exhibition of 150 of the finest pieces in Howard's collection. This show, which was co-sponsored and developed by Washington State University and the Smithsonian Institution Exhibition Service, had opened the year before (in November, 1982). Ultimately, the show was seen in all parts of North America.

I also found out that Howard was not on the faculty at Washington State University as I had been informed but, in fact, was one of my colleagues at the University of Washington. He was, I would soon learn, a gifted artist, a popular professor of ceramic art and, most importantly for me, the leading expert on Art Deco Noritake. His collection was huge (the 150-piece traveling show was a mere fraction of his holdings) but his knowledge about the Noritake Company and their Art Deco luster or fancy wares was even greater.

Howard gave me a copy of the exhibition catalog when we met for the first time in January, 1984. We talked for hours on that and many other occasions. He always seemed to enjoy looking at and commenting about the pieces in my collection. Most of his remarks were positive and, accordingly, both my confidence and my collection grew. I also discovered, however, that Howard could be, among other things, impish, irreverant, and iconoclastic. I thus came to appreciate that, with him, it often was almost impossible to be sure whether what he said was his true opinion or merely one of his wild verbal games.

There were, however, some things about Howard's viewpoint about which there can be no doubt. He had a truly *maniacal passion* for Art Deco Noritake, he was convinced that such porcelains, which he loved so much, were not "high art" but, instead, were a bare notch or two above pure "kitsch" (a "fact" in which he took considerable delight, especially among those who seemed, in his view, to take Noritake lusterware too seriously), and he knew what Art Deco was.

Unfortunately, this last claim does not mean that he wrote nice straight-foward diagnostic manuals or gave learned lectures telling how to identify and define the stylistic features of Art Deco Noritake. Neither does it mean that what I am saying here is basically his view (readers who want his view will find a brief version of it in the catalog of his show) or that he would agree with what I will say (indeed, I am almost positive he would disagree with much of it if, for no other reason, than for the love of a good argument).

I mention these things not only to acknowledge my debts to Howard but also to point out that he, like so many lovers of Art Deco or any other distinctive artistic tradition, mostly told people about it indirectly. In his case, his comments about my collection were a great help. I also learned much about it from him personally for he was completely wrapped up in the style; indeed, he literally wore it and lived in it. For example, he liked to provoke people by, among other things, wearing outrageously funky neckties from the 1930s and 1940s. He also had a massive collection of wild Deco-inspired modernist Hawaiian sport shirts. His home, which was quite modest in size but stunning in its overall impact, was filled with museum-quality Art Deco furnishings of all sorts. Knowing and visiting him was like attending a walking and walk-in seminar on Art Deco (and its aftermath).

What you will read here, therefore, is an amalgam; it is a mix of knowledge derived from my personal experiences and prejudices, from my exposure to the views of experts like Howard Kottler and others, and from a bit of reading on Art Deco that I have done. All of this is leavened by my professional interest, as a cultural anthropologist, in the general question of style as manifested in the historical development of cultural traditions, of which Art Deco can be considered an example.

## The Historical Roots of Art Deco

Except for the most basic facts about the history of the style (on which more in a moment), virtually everything about the Art Deco movement is still being debated by the experts. Indeed, hidden in the previous sentence is an innocent-looking but quite troublesome word that points directly to the heart of a rather significant issue within that debate. The word is the "the" in the phrase "the Art Deco developments" and the issue is how to delimit what in fact is not a single but, instead, is a diverse array of stylistic developments. Just as in Howard Kottler's life and home, Art Deco stylistic features could and can be found in almost any part of the human environment that was decorated – things as small as the type faces of books and as large as giant skyscrapers, as prosaic as restroom signs and as elegant as platinum and diamond jewelry, as workman-like as a drill chuck and as functional as a teapot.

The artistic, stylistic features of what we now know as "Art Deco" are rooted in certain intellectual, technological and social developments that first occurred in Europe and America in the years marking the transition from the nineteenth to the twentieth century. These nascent developments did not reach their fullest early flowering, however, until the years after World War I. Although it oversimplifies things greatly, one may gain a sense of what is meant by this claim about the roots of Art Deco by thinking of the monumental and, often, profoundly disturbing ideas emerging at about this time through the work of individuals like Einstein, Freud, Marx (via Lenin

and others), Picasso, Shaw, Edison, Ford, the Wright brothers, and Taylor (the famous "time-and-motion" expert). Relatively, sex and the unconscious, the revolutionary laws of history, cubism and primitiveness, wit and cynicism about whatever was most proper, electric lights and movies, assembly lines and stream-lining, powered flight, on-the-job-efficiency: these are but a few of the developments that would eventually shape, indeed, that would revolutionize the world in the first decades of this century.

These developments, and scores of others of nearly equal significance, provoked *radical* shifts away from what had been the norm. People like Freud, Einstein, Shaw, Marx, and Picasso questioned the unquestionable; their work undermined what most had long believed were timeless verities. Because of them, we literally see the world differently now than people did before these intellectual giants were on the scene. Individuals like Ford, Edison and the Wright brothers, on the other hand, actually did in steel and glass what others only dared to dream might be possible. Together, these intellectual and technological innovations resulted in massive shifts in the way people lived, worked and thought.

The mighty but ponderous engines of the early days of the industrial revolution of a century before were now beginning to reach previously unimagined speeds and to use stupifyingly large amounts of energy. At the same time, seemingly timeless axioms about our homes and families, dress and manners, mental and social life, laws and government were questioned. In some parts of the world, there were radical shifts in government; in others, new continents were being explored and colonial empires were established. The factories and offices in which we worked were fundamentally reshaped and basic physical changes were introduced in the design of the homes in which we lived. New moral standards were emerging along with fundamental social and legal changes regarding the rights and roles of women who, for the most part, continued to run those redesigned homes. And, there even were profoundly new conceptions of the very nature of the human mind.

Trends in the decorative and "high" arts reflected these dramatic social and technological developments of the early twentieth century. Artists too were searching for what, in time, came to be called the "moderne." The roots of these future trends and fads, it is important to note, were well underway by the first decade of this century and, one may speculate, could have reached full flower in the decade of the teens had it not been for the "war to end all wars." Therefore, the common claim that Art Deco was a "between the wars" phenomenon is, at best, a convenient oversimplification.

It is true, however, that it was simply impossible to mount a really large-scale international exposition oriented to the decorative arts in Europe until well after the war. Such a show had been planned for years but not until 1925 was it possible to hold the event. The main venue for that exposition was in Paris and it was, to put it mildly, a huge success. For decades, it literally changed the way the decorated world looked. Its impact was especially great in the United States. Large portions of the many exhibits were seen – *and paid attention to* – in all parts of the country.

Forty years later, however, its role in the history of the decorative arts was not well known except to specialists. This would change radically in 1966, however. In that year, the Musee des Art Décoratifs in Paris held an exhibition focusing on the decorative arts of the 1920s. That show, which recalled with great affection the 1925 Exposition Internationale des Arts Décoratifs et Industriels Modernes, had a most imposing name: Art Deco/Bauhaus/Stijl/Esprit Nouveau – a name that the press, in its own inimitable way, boiled down to "Art Deco": The phrase took hold and thus was born, for good or ill, a simple name for what is in fact a complex array of stylistic developments that took root during the first and flowered during, roughly, the next three decades of this century.

Because of the duration, fecundity and complexity of the stylistic ideas in the diverse, multi-national movements we now lump under the "Art Deco" rubric, it is almost certain that any attempt to say, in general, what Art Deco "is" or what the elements of the style are can (and should) be challenged. Even so, there are some qualities and features of the style that must be mentioned – if for no other reason than because they are so relevant to the Art Deco porcelains produced by the Noritake Company.

One of these, to start with but one of the more important examples given our purposes, is the way surfaces were treated. There were diverse developments but perhaps the most striking was the tendency to create radiant, mirrorlike surfaces through the lavish use of bright lacquers, highly polished exotic hardwoods such as ebony, and the application of various inlays such as brass and mother-of-pearl. Surfaces were not only embellished with suns complete with vibrant rays but also glistened from being covered with such new metals as aluminum and stainless or chrome-plated steel. To me, it seems transparent that the luster finish on the Noritake porcelains of the 1920s and 1930s reflects this trend.

Another trend during this period, especially in the United States, was the concern for efficient function and the love of powerful machines. This resulted in the virtual glorification of regular shapes, such as circles, triangles and squares, both because they had a strong, powerful look in and of themselves, and because it was felt such shapes could more easily be manipulated in the new mass-production processes. And, it seemed, everything was not only to be mass-produced but also, to as much an extent as possible, "*man*ufactured" – i.e., remade to reflect new conceptions of both "man" (especially "woman") and "nature." Scores of Art Deco works – everything from New York City skyscrapers to Noritake tea cups – show clear signs of these concerns.

A seemingly contradictory but in fact quite complementary development was an enthusiasm for the unfamiliar, the exotic, the irregular, the savage, the jazzy, the speedy, and the "distorted." Little if anything was taken at face value any longer. There were new perspectives, new angles of vision, new sources of inspiration; new places, cultures and destinations were discovered that enriched the Euro-American artistic world like never before. Even archaeologists got into the act by opening to our gaze previously great cultures and time periods that, up to then were almost entirely unknown (King Tut, for example). These developments yield Art Deco works, including more than a few by the Noritake Company, that have designs giving the flavor of cultures distant in both time and space.

**Examples of Noritake Art Deco Porcelains**

Studying the histories of recognized Art Deco masterpieces and consulting authorities regarding rules, principles and abstract "theory" is fine (indeed, it can be very helpful) but there is no substitute, especially in the arts, for looking long and hard at examples. A picture really is worth a thousand words. So, instead of reeling off boring lists of Art Deco stylistic features, I move directly to a consideration of some of the Noritake pieces pictured in this book. My goal will be to use them to discuss some things about the Art Deco style that collectors of Noritake may find interesting and useful to think about. Before doing so, however, I must make one additional rather important comment.

Although many collectors are interested in descriptions of an art style, and may even compile lists of its key elements for use when examining potential examples, it would be a *serious mistake for collectors to apply such knowledge in a mechanical fashion*, especially when making purchase decisions. We are, after all, talking about an art, not a science. Thus, at each and every purchase possibility, collectors should ask themselves: *"Do I really really like this piece?"* If the answer to this question is not a definite "yes," then you should not purchase the piece *for your collection.* I emphasize the last three words in the previous sentence because there most assuredly are reasons to buy a piece that one does not like. For example, one may do so in order to sell or trade the piece to other collectors for there really is wisdom in the adage which says that one person's trash is another's treasure.

Keeping this precautionary comment in mind, let us turn to the examples. For the sake of discussion, I present the examples in four groups: (1) pieces illustrating one or another of the more abstract aspects or relatively specialized features of the style, (2) pieces illustrating Art Deco's use of abstraction and stylization, (3) pieces exhibiting asymmetry and other general aspects of Art Deco design and, (4) pieces featuring motifs generally associated with one or another of the various strands of the Art Deco movement. This is done, it must be stressed, simply to facilitate this presentation of the material. There are several other ways these materials could and perhaps should be organized and, as the alert reader will quickly sense, many of the Art Deco pieces pictured in this book could easily appear in several of these groups. Also, although I will comment on many pieces, I do not discuss all the Art Deco items pictured in this book. There simply was not the space to do so.

## Group 1: Pieces Illustrating Abstract Elements of the Style

We will begin by considering extreme cases of non-substantive or "abstract" elements of the Art Deco style. Specifically, we will consider the matter of color, the shape of the porcelain blank and finish. Several colors had a certain vogue during the 1920s and 1930s and are intimately associated with the Art Deco style. Perhaps the best known of these are various shades of green (especially a pale or mint green and a deep forest or hunter green), a strong chrome yellow, a kind of light orange known as "Tango," a powerful blue known as "Lanvin" blue (after its popularization through its extensive use by the famous perfume company), and chrome (or silver)

itself.

By far, the most common luster colors on Deco Noritake porcelains are (variants or copies of "Lanvin"?) blue and several in the tan-orange ("Tango") range. Because these colors were used so widely by the Noritake Company, however, I think it would be inappropriate to use color alone as the grounds for calling a Noritake piece "Deco." I will not, therefore, attempt to use the color of the *luster* alone as a basis for identifying Deco items in this book even though a case can be made, as noted above, that a key feature of many wonderful Art Deco artworks is the creation of bright, metallic surfaces.

There are some pieces of Noritake, however, where the color itself is one of the primary bases for marking the item as a Deco item. Two of the best examples shown in this book are plates 606 and 1143. These are excellent Art Deco pieces for two main reasons: (1) color (the mint or light green) and (2) shape (particularly the layered look of the cream and sugar, and the basically square shape of the saucer). I am sure there are exceptions but, even so, it is not too far-fetched to say that virtually any Noritake with that particular shade of green would be a Deco piece.

Some other fine examples are the bowls in plates 788–790. That shade of green, as well as the yellow and chrome or silver detailing (especially on the piece in plate 789), marks these pieces as being solidly in the Deco style. The *shape* of these bowls, like the cream and sugar in plate 606 and the saucer of the set in plate 1143, also contributes significantly to the "Deco-ness" of these pieces (in this regard, see also the bowl in plate 671).

Another strong feature of Art Deco design was the bold use of quite regular geometric features: triangles, circles, and squares. Nevertheless, dramatic angular bowls, like the ones mentioned in the previous paragraph which combine these basic geometric shapes and, thus, have a distinctly Deco *shape*, do not appear to have been commonly made by the Noritake Company, at least so far as we know now. (Notice, too, the abstract floral motif in the bottom of the bowl in plate 790; it is an example of a design theme that I will discuss in some detail shortly.)

Many fine Art Deco pieces of Noritake porcelain may be so considered for reasons that, to some, seem odd – namely, the use of triangles in borders and wavy lines and/or bands or stripes consisting sometimes of parallel lines or accent colors (including chrome or silver). Triangles were an important Art Deco motif – if not inspired by, then certainly most awesomely displayed at the top of the Chrysler Building in New York City. There are not all that many Noritake pieces with this triangular motif but, with few if any exceptions, all those that do have them are rather striking Deco items. For example, consider the jam jar in plate 586 (which is, by the way, next to another beautiful piece, that on grounds of color and abstractness of design, is a Deco gem) and the bowls in plates 697–698 and plate 743.

Examples of the use of bold swirling or wavy ribbon-like bands are somewhat more common than the triangles and are a fairly important Art Deco stylistic feature. Generally, this motif appears to be intended to convey or express through the organization of the overall design something that was of great import to people of the 1920s and 1930s: speed (of the non-chemical variety). Given the rapid advances in powered flight, the development of genuinely powerful motor cars and the utilization on a wide scale of hugely powerful, streamlined train engines, it is fair to say that the people of that day were "hooked" on speed. Sometimes, therefore, bands of the sort being referred to here are called "speed-stripes."

It is difficult to convey a sense of speed and motion in all the arts except for the theatrical ones (drama, dance, cinema, television, and the like). In Noritake porcelains, a feeling of motion and speed does emerge through the use of ribbon-like bands of color and design detail. For example, consider the sandwich plate in plate 1024, the vases in plates 1366 and 1367 or the basket in plate 1388; consider also a similar ribbon or speed-stripe motif as it appears on the items in plate 826. Sometimes, the stripe is incorporated into the design more directly, as for example, in the cake plate shown in plate 1245. Although that speed-stripe is also a stem, its abstractness and strength lend a strong sense of motion to the piece (compare it, in this regard, to the cake plate next to it).

Finally, please turn to plate 1400 and consider the vase shown there in light of the points just made. For three reasons discussed so far, it may be considered a strong Deco piece. First, the vase has a regular (square) geometric shape that is given added interest with the pointed, almost triangular corners at the top. There is, second, the use of what may be called Art Deco mint green and, third, the overall abstract, geometric design involving (basically) triangles.

This piece may also be used to introduce a fourth Deco feature – namely, the shading in the green that has the look, at least, of having been achieved by the use of an airbrush. Airbrushes have been known to humans for many tens of thousands of years as can be seen by looking at the hands of our distant ancestors outlined by this method on the walls of the caves of France and Spain. During the 1920s and 1930s, however, the use of airbrushes (or at least the development of the look of airbrushing) became not only common but an important mark of the general Art Deco surface treatment. There are not too many Noritake porcelains with this look, however. Even so, it must be considered, along with color and shape, as one of the hallmarks of the Art Deco style. In this book, some very nice Deco pieces with this airbrushed look are as simple as the cream and sugar, small lemon plates and bowls shown in plates 748, 773, 844, 959, and 963.

In some Noritake Art Deco pieces, the airbrush was used to *shade* color, usually from a zone with virtually no color at all to one that displays the color quite intensely. At times, however, the entire piece was given a cool, flat look by the use of an airbrush which, of course, completely eliminates brush strokes or the sense of variable paint thickness. Although there do not appear to have been many pieces with this look produced by the Noritake Company, some are shown in this book (e.g., see plates 1028, 1337, and 1339).

One other comment about color should be introduced at this point, even though it does not bear on the question of Art Deco style per se. I refer to the matter of the colors of Noritake lusters. As noted previously, the most common luster colors are blue and various tan-to-orange shades. Another common color is the so-called "mother-of-pearl" luster which is usually white with pink and blue highlighting. It can be found in several other shades, as well, (e.g., green, purple, and gray are known).

One of the more striking of these shades is a pale yellow which, at times, is sufficiently dark and solid-looking to warrant being considered, simply, as a yellow luster. On the basis of information available now, this can be considered to be the rarest luster found on Noritake porcelains.

Finally, there are also quite a few pieces in a distinctly green or, sometimes, somewhat gray-green luster. Often, Noritake pieces with this color of luster will show various flaws or signs of wear – e.g., splotchy areas where the color is uneven, and faint areas that appear to be worn. Although the requisite technical information is as yet unavailable to me, it appears there may have been incompletely solved technical problems with this luster color. Sometimes, the glaze appears to have been applied unevenly at the time of manufacture; at other times, it appears to be a surface that, during even moderate use, rapidly developed signs of wear. Indeed, I have seen a few green and gray-green luster pieces in which one could easily rub off the color completely using nothing more than a fingernail – something that is all but impossible with the other lusters.

## Group 2: Pieces Exhibiting Abstraction and Stylization

In Noritake Art Deco porcelains, the most common and, often, the most well-executed feature of the Art Deco style may be referred to as *abstraction* or *stylization*. By "abstraction" and "stylization," I mean that the main object in the overall design is depicted in a recognizable but still quite non-realistic manner. Often this was accomplished by artfully "distorting" the shape of the object in various ways. For example, the item may be simplified by leaving out even rather obvious and otherwise important "details" that traditionally would have been considered essential for a "good" "likeness." Or, at other times, the shape might be changed by making the object larger, smaller or more elongated than normal. In some cases, the colors, especially of living things, are different than, if not virtually the opposite of, what one would find in nature.

Consider, for example, the bowl in plate 661. It is obvious that the objects depicted are flowers and a butterfly but it is safe to say that, in nature, there is no butterfly or flower in that shape or with those colors. The green leaves on the stems of the flowers in this piece are, however, fairly realistic or at least are rendered in a relatively conventional manner. Because of this, some might question whether this is a Deco piece. As with most such cases, the answer tends to mix matters of taste with conception of the style. I personally think it would be a mistake to conclude that the relatively realistic leaves make this a non Deco piece. I would make the same claim regarding the fabulous punch bowl in plate 1009.

Even so, it may be instructive to compare the green leaves in these pieces with the leaves in the two bowls in plates 697 and 698 and with the leaf-like forms in the dish shown in plate 795. In these, the entire plants – leaves, stems, blossoms and even their overall "stance" and shape are clearly abstractions from nature. That is, it is quite clear, beyond any doubt whatsoever, that the artist who designed these bowls was not attempting to *depict* but, rather, to *suggest* flowers. These bowls are, thus, superb examples of Art Deco abstraction and simplification or stylization. Two other outstanding pieces with

these qualities may be seen in plates 690 and 710.

With these examples in mind, the reader should next look closely at the flower in the bowl shown in plate 704. Although rose experts are likely to disagree, my feeling is that a pink and white rose very much like the one depicted on that bowl could exist in nature. Thus, although it is a beautiful bowl, I do not consider it to be an obvious Deco piece (although, as I discuss later, it can conceivably be argued that pieces with such a bold overall design do have Deco qualities). While you are on that page, compare that rose to the flowers depicted on the bowl in plate 703 which is, in my opinion, a fine Deco design.

Finally, I cannot conclude this discussion of abstraction in Noritake Deco florals without mentioning the large bowl shown in plate 770. It is, in my opinion, an excellent piece that I think ought to be called "Deco." Certainly the forms depicted in it are abstract and fanciful (i.e., non-natural)– so much so, in fact, that one could predict that many collectors might even doubt that they are flowers at all. And they may well be right!

This piece can also serve as the basis for reminding readers of my opening remarks about using the comments here when buying Art Deco (or any other kind of) Noritake. Thus, although I have singled out this bowl as being exceptional because of its unusually abstract (though not at all simplified, on which more shortly) "flowers," I would hope that collectors who encounter it and feel that it is "ugly" would not feel compelled to add it to their collection simply because somebody has tauted its supposed virtues. This bowl, like any other, should be purchased for one's collection only if one really really likes it. (By the way, anyone who does not like the bowl but who sees one for sale should be sure, please, to let me know right away!!)

## Group 3: Pieces Exhibiting Asymmetry and Other Aspects of Art Deco Design

In general, those of the floral and landscape designs produced by the Noritake Company which can be called "Art Deco" achieve this status primarily by abstraction and stylization. Other features can and do contribute to a Deco look, however. I have in mind those features which, collectively, constitute the overall design or presentation of the flowers or other objects such as cottages, mountains, lakes, and the like. Often it is this overall design that really gives a piece its strong look and emotional effect or, as I like to put it, its "POW-er."

Typically, such pieces have a design that, overall, is asymmetrical. This asymmetry is usually achieved by clustering objects off center so that the weight of the design is unbalanced. At other times, certain elements will, in a sense, be permitted to intrude on an otherwise fairly balanced design, thereby giving the piece dynamic feeling. In this book, there are many pieces that have this POW-erful look and we have already mentioned some of them for other reasons.

I have found that many collectors I know do not particularly care for these pieces. Even those who do like them will often refer to such pieces guardedly as being "wacky" or "brazen." Those for whom the Art Deco style is far less appealing are usually more direct and refer to such pieces as "garish" or, more bluntly, as "ugly." The bowl discussed above (plate 770) is and (if not "the") instance of such a POW-erful Deco design. For me, it is difficult to imagine a design that, overall, could be more energetic, mind-stretching and imaginative. These quite jarring but often aesthetically rather satisfying effects are achieved by such techniques as the use of unusual color combinations, the bringing together of familiar shapes to "manufacture" completely unfamiliar "natural" objects, and the arrangement of these objects into multi-layered, swirling patterns.

With this in mind, we can return to the bowl shown in plate 661. Initially, we discussed the abstract and unnatural qualities of the flower blossom and the butterfly. Now we may look at the bowl from the standpoint of its overall design. There is, to put it simply, a lot going on in that bowl. The flowers go in at least three directions, the butterfly in yet another and the connecting stems and background dots of color give the piece, overall, a kind of energy that is both unmistakable and, for me at least, very satisfying.

Critics, I readily admit, might just as easily and even more convincingly say (a little condescendingly, too), that the effect is unpleasantly "busy" or "disorganized." I make this point not merely to acknowledge that, when it comes to art, different people have different preferences. Rather, I make the point as a way of reminding readers that Art Deco artists and designers saw the world in a new way. It was the age of the Charleston, not the waltz; it was jazz that was king. Porcelain designers were part of this new age and, as a result, we should expect that at least some pieces of Art Deco Noritake may be a bit unsettling, even 75 years later. The aim was to provoke, to stimulate, and to suggest energy, vitality, and power where previously the goal would have been to depict more placid themes and sylvan qualities.

Interestingly, the Noritake Company artists were able to produce these powerful effects even in relatively small and simple items that, I think, too many collectors overlook or down play. For example, consider the effect of the asymmetrical semi-circular zones around three of the four edges of the otherwise simple little candy dish in plate 736. And, while you are there, look at the way the layered and unbalanced arrangement of flowers in the bowl in plate 737 distinctly energizes the piece. The effect of this overall design can perhaps be seen more easily by comparing it with the design of the floral bowl in plate 741 which, while quite attractive, simply does not have the energy of the pieces in plates 736 and 737.

Just a few of the many other wonderful examples of the bold, POW-erful look of Art Deco design in this book are to be found (a) in plate 690, where the strength of the overall design is almost exceeded by the wonderfully abstract flowers themselves; (b) in the bowl in plate 721 where the flowers seem to be shooting out of each other; (c) in plate 726 where the speed stripe and wave-like elements give a strong feel of motion; (d) in the previously discussed piece shown in plate 795 where the shape of the bowl itself so beautifully reinforces the effect of the arrangement of the flowers; (e) the sandwich plate in plate 1024 where much of the asymmetry seems to come from the speed stripe, and (f) the vase in plate 1391 which has wonderfully asymmetrical, flowing design that both fits with and, in a satisfying way, fights the confines of the cylindrical shape that may well be thought of as the heart of this terrific Deco piece.

## Group 4: Pieces Featuring Motifs Generally Associated with the Art Deco Movement

So far, my primary goal has been to discuss the *elements* of the Art Deco style – the (often tacit) "rules" and various aspects of technique that, taken together, yield what may be referred to as the manner in which artists and designers depicted various things. Also, though to a lesser extent, I have considered what may be referred to as the cultural forces that induced many of these artists to work in this way. Now, I wish to consider some of the supposedly Art Deco *motifs* found on Noritake fancy wares of the sort shown in this book.

By way of overview, I suggest below that many so-called Noritake "Deco" pieces should perhaps be thought of as primarily 1920s in subject matter and not particularly Deco in style. Saying this does not, I hasten to add, make such pieces any less desirable for the serious collector of Noritake Art Deco nor does such a claim detract from their beauty or value. It simply is a comment about what we, as beholders, are seeing when we look at many pieces of Noritake made during the height of the Art Deco era – the mid-1920s and early 1930s.

To illustrate my point very briefly, we need only recall that there are, for example, many many Noritake porcelains from this period that, in one way or another, feature birds and houses. Few collectors would suggest, however, that all Noritake pieces with houses or birds on them are "Deco." Obviously, far more than subject matter needs to be taken into account when deciding whether or not a piece is Deco.

I make this really quite elementary point because I begin this discussion of Noritake Art Deco subject matter by making what some will think is at least an ill-considered if not sacrilegious remark: many Noritake lady pieces are not very Deco stylistically even though many of them may be described as Deco in subject matter. This contrast between style and subject matter may be illustrated by comparing the covered boxes in plates 1197 and 1199.

In part, I selected these two for discussion because they are rather similar and because most collectors would consider both to be rather good pieces. Indeed, one can say with great confidence that many Noritake collectors would want them and, consequently, that both would command substantial prices. Only the item in plate 1197, however, really shouts "Art Deco" to me. Even though the differences may seem small, the item in plate 1197 entails more abstraction, stylization, asymmetry, and other aspects of Art Deco design than the piece in 1199 (which I feel especially free to be "critical" of since it happens to be my piece – one that I am pleased to be able to say is a part of my collection, by the way). It (plate 1197) is, therefore, a stronger Deco piece, at least in my opinion.

To put it somewhat differently, I think it is useful to distinguish depictions of the style from depictions in the style. Both women are wearing clothing that, in terms of style, reflects the impact of Art Deco design principles (and other factors too numerous to mention here). As such, both pieces can be seen as depictions of Art Deco in that they record fashions inspired by that stylistic tradition which was, after all, pre-eminent at that time. The *manner* in which these fashion trends and the two women are depicted, however, is somewhat different. The woman in plate 1197 has been rendered in a more stylized, abstract and dramatic way than is the case for the woman in plate 1199. As such, the piece in plate 1197 is more than a record *of* the style; it is *in* that style, as well.

This admittedly somewhat subtle point should become clearer if the other two lady pieces on that page of this book are considered. As before, we may ask whether these ladies are depictions "of" or "in" the Art Deco style. More basically, we may also ask whether or not either of these wonderful items are "Art Deco" pieces and, why or why not. At this point, many collectors would interject and assert, understandably, that such questions are simply beside the point since both trays (plates 1196 and 1198) are exceptionally beautiful and would add greatly to any Noritake collection.

That is undeniably true and, like most collectors, I would be delighted if I owned either tray and deliriously happy if I owned both. Also, if granted on caveat, I would be willing to side with the majority and assert that these are indeed fine "Deco" pieces. The caveat is this: I would want to add that they are Deco only in the broad sense of the term. That is, they are not so much Deco in style as being a record of events that were important during the 1920s – events that were both influenced by and helped to produce what we think of now as the Art Deco style. In other words, these two trays, as fine as they are, are not so important for whatever Art Deco qualities they might have (and both have some; I return to this point shortly) but for the way they record developments that were socially significant in the 1920s, a period dominated, stylistically by Art Deco.

To some, of course, it may seem strange to call something "Deco" simply because it depicts a socially significant event of the period during which Art Deco was at or near its peak. And, if that was all there was to it, I think they would be correct. In these cases, however, these pieces, although only minimally Deco in style, can be considered "Deco in the broad sense because they record events that were the product of the very same social, philosophical, technological, and political forces that produced the Art Deco movement, more narrowly defined.

Thus, in plate 1196, we see (among other things) a woman who appears ready to attend one of the many elaborate high-society costume balls that were popular in the 1920s. Her costume, which arguably has Deco qualities because of the floral detailing, also resonates with the revival, during this period, of an interest in clowns – a development that was carried over into the world of high fashion. Similarly, in the tray depicting the skier (plate 1198; it is known among collectors as "Susy Skier"), we see a woman doing something that, prior to this period, women seldom did: ski. Many of the most desirable Noritake lady pieces are similar in that they show women doing things that, prior to the 1920s, were uncommon and/or scandalous (e.g., smoking; using make-up).

It is possible – indeed, it is quite useful – to think of the widespread use of make-up by women as having contributed to and been a product of the forces that shaped the Art Deco movement. It is this "fact" that makes it reasonable to consider many of the wonderful dresser dolls and powder jars with figural ladies shown in this book (e.g., plates 457–484), which in my opinion are usually minimally Deco in style, as Deco in the broad sense of the term. Those porcelains, in other words, are a record of key social developments of the Art Deco period. That they are not all equally Deco in style, however, can be seen rather easily by comparing plates 472 and 474. One of these, and I leave it to the reader to decide which it is, has far and away more Deco stylistic features than the other.

Thus and in summary (at least regarding the lady pieces), we may say that many of the very best and most famous Noritake lady pieces are not so much Deco in style as they are 1920s in subject matter. They are not in the style but of (or about) it. To take a new and quite dramatic example, the Noritake pieces influenced by the popular 1920s musical *Mme. Pompador* (e.g., plates 1152, 1174, 1207, 1211, 1226, and 1346 are among the most obvious in this regard. There are many other lady pieces which, although also much sought-after by nearly every serious Noritake collector, are not obviously or strongly in the Deco style. The reader is encouraged, here to make her or his own judgments regarding, for example, the ladies in plates 1148, 1149, 1155, 1159, 1215, 1225, 1232, 1239, 1345, 1348, 1351, 1355 and 1360.

Many pieces, however, are both in and of the style. The "Susy Skier" tray discussed above may be mentioned first as a piece that at least "comes close," primarily by virtue of the overall design – e.g., her placement on the tray, the stylized rendering of her skis (any skier will know instantly that she will have serious problems skiing down a hill wearing her skis the way she is), and the speed-stripe quality of her flowing scarf. The border of the piece has strong Deco qualities, as well.

There are, however, many lady pieces that I think can fairly be described as strongly in and of the Art Deco style (e.g., consider the ladies in plates 1145, 1154, 1158, 1165–66, 1169, 1170, 1178–79, 1185–86, 1220, 1222, 1224, 1262, 1304, 1309, 1353–54, 1356, 1357, 1361 and 1363). The piece that would get my vote as being most assuredly both in and of the Deco style is shown in plate 1201. I find it hard to imagine how one could get more of the Deco era into a piece that is more in a Deco style than has been accomplished in this elegant tray. It seems to have everything: boldness of colors, stylization, asymmetry and perhaps most importantly in this piece, vital subject matter. Would that I owned one!

## Summary and Conclusions

I have not said all that could and should be said about Art Deco as a style or about the pieces pictured in this book, Art Deco or otherwise. Indeed, I have not even come close to merely mentioning all of those that I think merit being called "Deco." What seems most important to me, at this point, is to emphasize two things. First, and as was noted several times in this essay, the Art Deco period is long, complex, international, and muti-cultural; it is, therefore, difficult if not impossible to give a finite list of the rules for identifying, precisely, what is and what is not a "Deco" artwork.

Second, and as was noted at least once in the above, there is a tendency to mix matters of style as conceived historically with matters of taste as viewed personally. In my opinion, however, this is not a bad thing. On the contrary, it would be a mistake for at least two reasons for collectors to buy by a "rulebook," even if one existed. In the first place, any book that claimed to have the rules of Art Deco down pat would have to be a bad book. Second, and more importantly, collectors ought to collect what they *like*.

In sum, I hope collectors will continue their pursuits primarily with passion and joy, not by rigidly adopting the standards of guidebooks and essays like this one. At the same time, however, it may prove to be helpful, while searching for Art Deco Noritake, to be on the lookout at the same time for ideas about Art Deco as a style. Finding the latter can be as satisfying as the former.

---

*Searching for Art Deco Noritake and the Elements of a Style: A Personal Account.* Copyright David H. Spain. All rights reserved.

*As noted in the credits to the previous essay, David Spain is, among other things, editor of* Noritake News — *the newsletter for collectors of and dealers in Noritake lusterware and other Noritake collectibles (excluding dinnerware). He is interested in hearing from all Noritake collectors, and especially those who love the Art Deco wares produced by the Noritake Company. Those readers interested in subscribing to the newsletter may write to the editor at 1237 Federal Avenue East, Seattle, WA 98102.*

## Selected Additional Sources on Art Deco and Related Matters

Duncan, Alastair. 1988. *Art Deco.* London: Thames and Hudson. (A small but very detailed book by comparison to many that are available. It covers all aspects of the style and has good illustrations, nearly all in black and white.)

Hillier, Bevis. 1971. *The World of Art Deco.* New York: E.P. Dutton.(Essentially a catalogue of what must have been a truly fabulous exhibition held at The Minneapolis Institute of Arts in 1971. The book has many fine illustrations, all in black and white, and useful historical information.)

Klein, Dan. 1974. *All Colour Book of Art Deco.* London: Octopus Books. (As the title says, this book has color photos and, although it may not be easy to find, will be worth it when you do. Try used bookstores. It is a small book but breathtakingly beautiful.)

Kottler, Howard. 1982. *Noritake Art Deco Porcelains.* Pullman, WA: Museum of Art, Washington State University. (This is the source, for now, on Art Deco Noritake porcelains. It has only a small number of photos, some in color and is out of print. It is, however, available and highly recommended for the serious collector. For information, write *Noritake News*.)

Labanov-Rostovsky, Nina. 1990. *Revolutionary Ceramics: Soviety Porcelain, 1917–1927.* New York: Rizzoli Publications. (This is not a book about Art Deco per se. It is, however, a beautiful book about one of the many artistic strands that was an inspirational part of this many splendored thing we call "the" Art Deco movement. The book is beautifully produced and, when examined carefully, will completely put to rest any lingering notion that Art Deco was invented in 1925 in Paris, although this is not at all the book's objective.)

McClinton, Katherine Morrison. 1986. *Art Deco: A Guide for Collectors.* New York: Clarkson N. Potter, Inc., Publishers. (First published in 1972, this book is pretty much as billed in the title. Some kinds of Art Deco items, such as buildings, are almost completely absent from this otherwise useful book. I suppose this is understandable since few of us can afford to collect buildings. Talk about your space problems!!)

Papadakis, Andreas C., ed. 1987. *The Post-Modern Object.* London: Art and Design. (This book also is not about Art Deco – obviously, given the title. It is included here because it will give the Art Deco Noritake collector a hint of things that have happened to and in the name of our beloved style since..., well, since the modern world was thought to have started to fall apart. The beautiful things in it – again, everything from buildings to teapots – will have a more familiar and appealing look than you might expect.)

Weber, Eva. 1985. *Art Deco in America.* New York: Exeter Books. (I think that if you could have only one of the books listed here, and you wanted a large book, both in number of pages and format, that has a little of everything – the diversity, scope, color, and history of Art Deco, including even some fine color photos of some of Kottler's greatest Noritake pieces, then this is the book.)

# Photographing Your Collection
## by: Polly Frye, M. Photog. Cr., CPP

**The Importance of Photographs**

Whether you own one or two pieces of Noritake, or a large collection, there comes a time when you want some photographs. This is especially important for insurance purposes, should you have breakage or theft. Never file your negatives and photographs in the same place. If your collection is very valuable, you may want to store your negatives in a safe deposit box at your bank or at least in a fireproof box at home. 35mm negatives do not take up much room and would give you the peace of mind to know that you have proof of your valuables.

Having photographs to carry with you when you are searching for a piece or pieces to match a certain set can be invaluable. There are times when you may want to ask another person to be on the lookout for something for you and it makes it much easier for them to see just what you are trying to match. After all there are many different designs and colors.

**The Basic Setup**

Since much of the Noritake is highly glazed, this creates more problems than your average china and porcelain when it is being photographed. This could be a very complex process, building a plastic tent and using flood lights and filters. The average person does not have the knowledge or desire to get this involved. There is a much simpler way and I shall attempt to explain it to you.

On a cloudy or overcast day select a spot near a window. A north window may be best even on a bright day. On the other hand, on a bright, sunny day you may find the right spot on an inside wall. Put a sturdy card table or other flat top piece of furniture near a window or against the inside wall. Before you set up, put a piece to be photographed in place and see that there are no shadows or only slight ones. Light shadows can be eliminated by placing a large piece of white art board on the shadow side of the piece to reflect light back into the shadow area. A chair with a flat bottom and high back could be used if you are only photographing a couple small pieces, but for sets you will probably need a larger surface. A piece of heavy cardboard will serve to form a back to attach the art paper or cloth onto. If you have a window

close to a corner, you may be able to use the wall for your backdrop. The window light will be coming in from the side which will give roundness and/or texture to the piece. Tape the piece of colored art paper or cloth to the top of the cardboard, wall or chair back depending on which you are using. Bring it down over the surface of the table and over the edge forming a continuous curve; letting it hang loose at the back with no crease where it hits the table.

The color of the background should be in contrast to the piece to be photographed. I use a lot of black behind light objects but some people do not like the dark background. The use of a white background has some advantages as it will reflect light on the underneath side of objects with rounded bottoms as with saucers, etc. There are some synthetic fabrics that do not have textures and do not wrinkle which are excellent for backgrounds. You must be sure the cloth is wrinkle free if you go this route. Velvets are nice but do have a shiny surface that you may object to in the finished photograph.

I really prefer to photograph my porcelain outside. But this may not be practical with highly glazed pieces because you may pick up some reflections. An overcast day is ideal but you can work in open shade as well. By that, I mean the side of the house and not under trees where patches of light may come through the leaves. You can use the side of a building to attach your background onto, using the same method as described for inside. It is possible to hold a piece of white cardboard between the light source and the object to cut out the hot spots or reflections. You can see these as you look through the camera and many times just moving a little up and down or side to side can eliminate them. The angle of the camera is very important to emphasize certain areas on a piece that you want to show. Move your camera around and soon you will learn the best angle.

**The Equipment**

You should have a single lens reflex 35mm camera. This will enable you to look through the lens and see exactly what you are recording on the film. There are many good cameras on the market; Nikon, Cannon, Leica, and Minolta, to name a few. But many of the professionals that I know, use Nikon. At the present time, I am using a Nikon 2020 with 50mm f1.9 lens. It has both automatic or manual exposures and focus. This way you have complete control over your exposures and focus. A good lens is a MUST, the body is not as important but you will want one that gives you automatic exposures. At this point, I could go into f/stops and manual exposures. However, if you know nothing about photography, I feel this would only be confusing to you. I promised to keep it as simple as possible and with automatic exposure you will get good results. Later when you become more experienced you may want to try the different f/stops. Even as a professional, I find that I use only the automatic exposure for this type of photography. If you do not have a good camera, you can plan to spend at least $400.00 for a good quality camera, lens and lens shade. The lens shade serves two purposes: 1) it protects your lens and 2) it helps to keep light flare off of the camera lens. In order to photograph small objects you will need either a +2 or +3 close-up filter to put on front of your lens or a 2x Macro-Focusing Teleconverter which goes between your camera body and the lens. Either of these should give you satisfactory results for small pieces. Remember you only need one or the other and not both.

If you are going out to buy a new camera, go to a local dealer who is knowledgeable and will help you select the best buy for your money. Most importantly someone who will take the time and be available to help you learn how to operate your camera. This will most likely be a camera shop that deals with professionals.

You will need a sturdy tripod in order to get good results. Most people can not hand hold a camera to get the sharpness that you desire. It is also very helpful to center your objects in the frame. You will want the object to be photographed to fill the frame in the camera. But keep in mind that a little of what you see will be cropped in the printing, so don't overcrowd.

## Type of Film

Before you buy film you must decide if you want prints or slides. If you choose to have prints, slides can be made from negatives very successfully. However, prints that are made from slides are not of the best quality. Colors are seldom as they appear in the prints. Any good quality film is all right with speeds of 100 or 200. The faster speeds do not produce the best results. I use a lot of Fuji film as I find the colors a little sharper. Above all, never use flash, as you have no way to keep the glare from your object.

Developing the film is very important, also. Many times poor photographs are the result of the processing and not a result of your ability to take a good photo. Select a good lab, cheap processing rarely pays off when you want the colors to be true as possible. If you deal with the same lab you should be able to establish a good working relationship that will prove to be beneficial to you and the lab as you buy your film and supplies from them. Another tip that you may find helpful: should you feel that you will need more than one set of photos, order two sets when you have the film developed. It will cost less than to reorder another set later and in most cases the first run prints are best. There is no logical explanation for this but it just happens to be true in many cases.

## An Assistant

You will find it a tremendous help to have an assistant, especially if you set out to photograph a lot of Noritake at one time. Someone that you can trust to handle the pieces and bring them to you. You will do well to sort them ahead of time in order to photograph all the pieces that are to be placed against a certain color background. You will not want to change backgrounds any more times than is absolutely necessary. Allow plenty of time, accidents happen when you get in a hurry. A chipped or broken piece can be very costly.

Also, when photographing sets vs. individual pieces, sort them as much as possible, doing all the sets together and the individual pieces at one time. When you have a lot of pieces in one set, you may want to photograph the entire set and then photograph just one or two pieces to show more detail.

It is an excellent idea to photograph each new piece when you acquire it. You will find it much simpler to do it before you put them in your inventory or collection. If you must wait until later it means you must handle them again. It really doesn't take too much time or require too much effort to set up, once you get the hang of it. And if you are only photographing a piece or so, you should not need an assistant.

You have invested a lot of money in your collection; now you should be willing to invest in a good camera and lens in order to have good photographs. In the long run, it will be much less expensive than hiring a professional, not to mention the convenience of doing it in your own home.

I hope this will encourage you to produce some nice photographs of your Noritake. Some that you will be proud to show your friends and fellow collectors.

*A step-down arrangement can be especially helpful in photographing sets with lots of pieces.*

*Showing outside setup using tripod and cloth attached to a wall.*

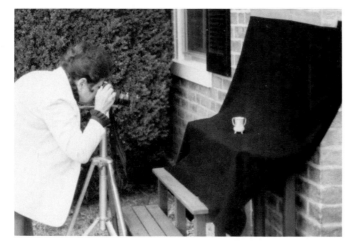

*Showing closer view of setup using tripod and cloth attached to a wall.*

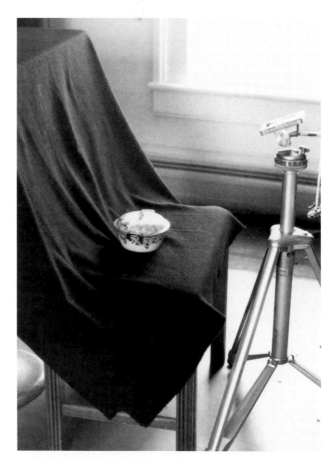

*Another view of the inside setup. Note the problem that can happen using cloth vs a poster board background. Photographing straight into the item will eliminate much of this.*

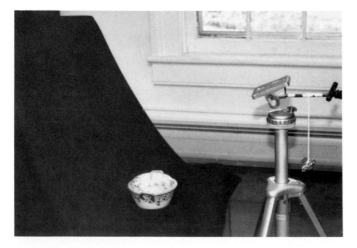

*Inside setup using window light on the side. Tripod necessary to insure sharp negatives.*

# Buying and Selling Through the Mail

Buying through the mail can be an easy way to purchase an item. You don't have to shop for hours or go to antique shows, shops, flea markets, auctions, or estate sales. You can sit in the comfort of your own home and someone else does all the legwork for you.

Many ads for collectibles are featured in trade magazines and newspapers. First thing you should do is read the ad carefully. Call if you can to get more information but keep in mind the different time zones. Someone in California might not appreciate a phone call at 6:00 a.m. in the morning! Make sure that there are return privileges and that you understand them correctly. Ask for a discount in price – remember nothing ventured, nothing gained. If you change your mind after putting a reserve on an item over the phone be courteous enough to call back and cancel. If you are in doubt about the item, ask for photos and then return them promptly.

If you do not call be sure to print or write your letter legibly and always include a SASE (self-addressed stamped envelope). The seller may wait until your personal check clears before mailing you the item. If you are in a hurry you can always send a money order or certified check to speed things up. Give the seller correct shipping instructions. If you have doubts about the item write and ask for a photo, again enclosing a SASE. A SASE will be used to mail you the photos or an answer that the item was sold or return excess postage if the seller is requesting that you pay for it. If you have a tax number also be sure to include this.

After receiving the item inspect it carefully. If the piece is not to your liking you should pay postage both ways, if the dealer has misrepresented the item then I feel he/she should pay postage both ways.

When selling through the mail include your phone number if possible. It helps to have an answering machine turned on if you are not at home to take your calls. Be sure to be courteous and follow up on these calls.

Be prepared to send good clear photos if requested. List the items correctly noting any damage or wear.

After the buyer's check has cleared, mail the item promptly.

Agree ahead of time on how the merchandise will be shipped, by mail or UPS. Remember that UPS does not deliver to a post office box. Also decide upon ahead of time who pays for the postage.

Wrap the item securely, using plastic chips, shredded paper, or even popcorn as a filler around the piece. Double box and use strapping tape on the outside box. Include an address card inside.

Insure the item and offer return privileges. Three to five days after the item is received by the purchaser seems to be a reasonable amount of time. If you have asked for postage money be sure to return any excess.

# A Dealer's Viewpoint
## on Noritake prices and trends
### by Dennis Burnikas

As a dealer, it is essential to have books on the antiques and collectibles I normally buy and sell. It's been said that "a house without books is like a room without windows. There's no view to the outside world." And for me, and for most of the dealers I know, maintaining such a library is about the only practical method we have for obtaining adequate information for the many collecting specialties of our customers and, thereby, staying in business.

Every collector I know loves to tell about those times when he has bought a piece at a bargain price. As collectors, this is one of the most enjoyable facets of spending a day, roaming around at a flea market or an antique mall. From a dealer's perspective, however, such stories often hit a sensitive nerve for the collector's bargain had to be the dealer's perspective, however, such stories often hit a sensitive nerve for the collector's bargain had to be the dealer's loss.

Both collectors and dealers know that, as the old saying goes "you win a few and you lose a few." As long as that is the general pattern, things tend to work out all right. But for the dealer who mostly "loses a few" it usually means they are not in business very long. Thus, I hope it can be appreciated that we need price guides and collector books in order to "win a few" and, thereby, stay in business.

I readily acknowledge that there are dealers who take price guides literally and who use them religiously. My sense is, however, that most such dealers are beginners who, in using the price guides in this way, are, in effect, admitting that they know virtually nothing about a particular collecting field other than what the book says. In fact, when setting prices, most of the experienced dealers I know take a great many factors into account. Indeed, in some instances, the price guide turns out to be one of the least important factors.

Noritake collecting (1921–41) is a relatively new field. As a consequence, although material in Book I was vitally important to both dealers and collectors, I often found that the pieces I had were not pictured. Sometimes there were similar items (the same porcelain blank with a different decoration) but in other cases (and as a dealer I often found myself wishing this had happened more often) a piece might be completely unlike anything shown in the book (many items of this sort are, of course, now included in Book II). This can often make it difficult to use a price guide to establish prices.

When a piece is not pictured, one thought that often comes to mind, especially as a dealer is "Maybe I've got a rare piece on my hands." Usually, this is a happy thought because quite often – but by no means always – that means the profit potential is higher. But it is not easy to decide when something is truly "rare," especially in a field like Noritake, where there are few records as to the quantities produced. Sometimes, pieces that are thought to be rare and that, as a result, command high prices, turn out to not be rare. In part this is because the high prices lead others (usually not collectors) who have such pieces to part with them, thus putting more of them on the market. At first, prices may stay high but before too long, they will drop. Prices tend to soften when pieces are more readily available and so those who follow the price guide strictly may well price themselves out of the market (and, ultimately, out of business).

Another reason a price guide can't be used blindly is that tastes change. Sometimes these changes can be both rapid and dramatic. For several years, for example, figural Noritake was the "hottest" seller. It seemed, that there would be no end to the demand for such pieces. And the prices dealers charged reflected this intense demand. But, apparently, the sages are right: all good things do seem to come to an end. In the last few years, the rate of increase in the prices of figurals has slowed considerably. Those dealers not aware of this may find their figurals sitting unsold for long periods if they have set their prices strictly in accordance with the price guide inflation.

As a dealer I not only take into account the price I have to pay for a piece when establishing a selling price, I also consider (1) popularity or style, (2) the aesthetic or artistic merit of piece, and (3) rarity.

Popularity and style are important considerations but, as noted above, tastes change and often quite rapidly. I try, therefore, to keep things moving by making prices on popular styles reasonable – mostly because I don't want to be stuck with a piece that was "yesterday's rage." Art Deco Noritake is very popular right now. It seems that the demand is strong enough to say that prices for such pieces can reliably be set fairly high. I have been around long enough, however, to know that this too shall pass. Not next year, at least not in my opinion, but who knows what will be "hot" five or ten years down the road.

The artists who designed and the crafts people who produced and decorated Noritake porcelains were very talented people. Even so, not every design that was produced is extremely well executed. Consequently, a dealer (and a collector) must take into account the artistic merit of a piece. Some very fine designs were poorly produced; on the other hand, some significant artistic efforts were sometimes lavished on rather ho-hum designs. In the long run, beautifully produced pieces with excellent designs are the most certain to retain their value. Prices do – and should – reflect this fact.

A piece can be rare in two ways: it can be "absolutely" rare when there are, in absolute numerical terms, "very few" such pieces or it can be "relatively" rare when there are far more collectors who want a given piece than there are pieces available. With Noritake, it is very difficult to say which pieces are "absolutely" rare since so little is presently known about the number of pieces produced or the number in collections. As for items that are "relatively" rare, there appear to be quite a few in that category in the Noritake field today. There are, in other words, lots of pieces that a great many collectors are just aching to get their hands on and that, so far anyway, have not turned up in any quantity. Whether such pieces will turn out to be "absolutely rare" remains to be seen. (And don't forget: a rarity is not easy to define or identify and moreover, it is not, by itself, grounds for a high price. Even a true one-of-a-kind piece will not garner a high price if it lacks style and/or is poorly designed and produced.)

These factors, plus the knowledge one gains after managing to stay in this business for a few years plus the information in a book like this one will help me to establish an asking price. At that point, the next move is yours. And remember: "it never hurts – either you or me – to ask!"

*Note from JVP – The two-piece covered box shown in this photo is a wonderful find for any dealer or collector and the piece de resistance as far as I'm concerned!*

# A Collector's Potpourri of Information

Porcelain has a bell-like sound when tapped. It is smooth to the touch and the glaze does not flake off. The degree of its translucency is due to the amount of glass in the fired body. Light passes through glass – the more glass – the greater percentage of transmitted light and the greater the translucency. Biscuit firing is done at about 950°C, glost firing is done at over 1400°C, and decoration firing is done at 850°C – 1250°C.

If you find a long raised bar shape or star shape on the bottom of an item it's called a "spur" mark and is there only to give the item strength when it is being fired. It is not a backstamp and should not affect the price of the piece.

Collectors of Nippon era (1891–1921) pieces find shaving mugs, egg warmers and mustache cups but rarely do we find these same type items made in the 1921–41 time period. Pierced berry bowls, calling card trays, hat-pin holders, pancake servers, spitoons, sugar cube holders, whiskey and wine jugs, knife rests and cinnammon stick holders are also uncommon and rarely found. But we do now find bridge sets, powder puff boxes, wall pockets, sugar berry and cream sets, and seasoning sets. Figural finials are found on a number of the items, also the lavish use of luster reminiscent of many of the popular Czecho-slovakian wares.

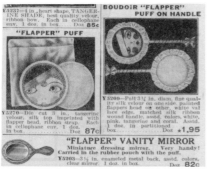

*Illustration #1*

Pieces decorated in an Art Deco style became popular. People of this time period seemed to be uncluttering their lives of extra dishes but wanted their items more whimsical. Powder puff boxes were in vogue and were often sold with decorated puffs displaying flapper style designs, (see illustration #1). Many of our favorite Noritake pieces featuring the flapper were copies of French designs as indicated in a January 1928 Butler Bros. catalog ad featuring brooches, (see illustration #2).

In the 1921–41 period we do not find the tapestry decor used, very few moriage or wedgwood style pieces, or incised wares of gold or silver overlay. Coralene is non existent. When we do find some of these type decorations it is safe to assume they were manufactured in the early 1920s.

Portrait silhouettes became more popular at this time (see photo #1, page 39) as well as figural type wares (photo #2, page 40). I call this the "fun" period.

The discovery of King Tutankhamen's tomb in Egypt in November of 1922 had an influence on wares of this time period. This news flashed around the world with great excitement. There was now a hunger for things that were Egyptian in decoration and the Japanese quickly adapted some of these patterns on Noritake wares. Triangles represent mountains and wavy lines are water. Set, the brother and slayer of Osiris is shown with the head of an animal. We find portraits of Egyptian women, pyramid scenes as well as palm trees, sailboats, Nile scenes, and men on camels.

*Illustration #2*

Today's collector likes to match up pieces bearing the same pattern (Photos #3 & 4, page 40; and photo 5, page 41). The tree in the meadow pattern is a favorite with collectors and the man on a camel is another. It's also interesting to see how collectors display their pieces. One collector may have wall pockets displayed everywhere (photo #6, page 41) while another may just keep filling up the china cabinets (photo #7, page 41). Some prefer to group their pieces together such as vases in one spot, bowls in another.

Collectors are often confused in the identification of their items. They don't know the difference between a plaque and a plate or a humidor and a biscuit jar. A plaque was intended to be hung on the wall and will have holes for this purpose on the reverse side. A plate or large platter will not. A charger is a large wall plaque, at least 14" in diameter. A humidor may sometimes look like a cracker or biscuit jar but will have a hole on the inside cover where a sponge was originally placed. Chambersticks have handles, candlesticks do not. A condensed milk container will have a hole in the bottom to push out the can whereas that wouldn't be very good in a jam jar. They look similar but are not. The difference between an individual size teapot and a syrup will be the steam hole found on the cover of the teapot. A pancake server often looks like a covered butter dish but will have pierced holes in the top for steam. It will also have no insert (this was placed over ice to keep the butter cold) and will be larger in size.

Many of the Noritake pieces were originally sold through mail order catalogs and through the use of salesman's sample books. The old illustrations in these books are wonderful to look at and today individual pages from some of these books often sell for more than the piece displayed. Collector friends of mine have had these pages framed and proudly display them in their homes as works of art. The pages contain illustrations that have been hand drawn and painted with water colors by the artists

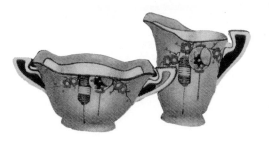

who most likely decorated the pieces at the factory in Nagoya. Many of these pages have pencil notations of numbers and descriptions such as :

    175/504 salt and pepper, 180 box
    135/502 ashtray, 90 pcs
    101/504 tea set, 24 sets
    102/504 cake set, 48 sets
    126/501 condiment set, 60 pcs
    101/520 tea set, 24 sets
    142/500 handled basket, 48 pcs
    117/500 open sugar and creamer, 60 pcs
    126/502 condiment set, 60 sets
    109/503 sandwich set, 36 sets
    119/500 spooner, 48 pcs
    131/509 candlestand, 48 sets
    134/502 Pierrette ashtray, 40 pcs
    125/506 salt and pepper, 200 box
    101/514 tea set, 36 sets
    103/507 berry set, 36 sets
    131/507 comport, 36 sets

Part of the numbering system probably refers to a pattern name and the amount either refers to how much was

ordered or how much was the minimum order such as 180 pieces or pairs in a box.

The store buyer knew exactly what he would be receiving and the salesman didn't have to travel with

the actual samples. Some of the pages will show only part of a plate or bowl decorated, others will be found with sev-

*Photo #1. Portrait silhouettes.*

eral patterns and styles for a particular piece shown such as a sugar shaker. Some show a side view, some a top view.

Figurals are always exciting to find and an interesting one is the Oriental figurine, its hair in a queue (a long braid) down its back. I'm not sure if the one displayed is male or female. The piece is 7" tall and bears the green M in wreath mark #27. Note in photos 8–10 (pages 41 & 42) how the artists painted each differently.

Some of these figurines have been found with a hole drilled in and it's believed that a number were intended to be used as lamp bases.

Many times individual salts have become separated from the rest of the original set. The tray in photo #11 (page 42) has an M in wreath #27 backstamp but the salts are marked with just the word JAPAN while some are marked Made in Japan. When separated from the tray we're not always sure when we find them if they fall within the 1921–41 period. The individual salts in photos #12–14 (page 42) are now alone from the rest of their sets but I do believe these are from this era.

Some of the Art Deco designs we find were adaptions from old advertising posters and lithographs. In 1925 the play *Madame Pompadour* was produced by the Shubert Brothers in New York City. The sets were designed by Homer Conant and photo #15 (page 43) is an original lithograph (13½" x 9½") from this play. Madame Pompadour (1721–64) was the mistress of Louis XV, King of France. She was installed in the palace of Versailles and had great influence with Louis. She was also a patroness of the arts. Collectors will notice the similarity of this lithograph to the plate (photo #16, page 43) manufactured by the Noritake Company. It was copied almost exactly. About the only difference between the two is Homer Conant's signature. Photo #17 (page 43) is a close-up of this wonderful lithograph. It was found accidentally in an antique shop long before the matching plate was found and collectors may want to keep their eyes open for more such wonderful finds. It's nice to display the two side by side. Salesman's sample pages with matching items are another exciting addition to a collection.

Photos #18 & 19 (page 44) are Noritake items that closely resembles the lithograph but with some changes. This could possibly be a copy of another lithograph. Photo #20 (page 44) is a cardboard container for "Piquante" face powder by Colgate and Company of New York. This box is shown in the book *Commercial Perfume Bottles* by Jacquelyne J. Jones-North in a reproduction of a 1924 magazine advertisement. The box is 2¼" tall and 2⅞" wide. It is reminiscent of the designs found on other Noritake pieces and items such as this, although not Noritake porcelain, add a certain flair to a collection.

*Photo #2. Figural items.*

*Photo #3. Matching items.*

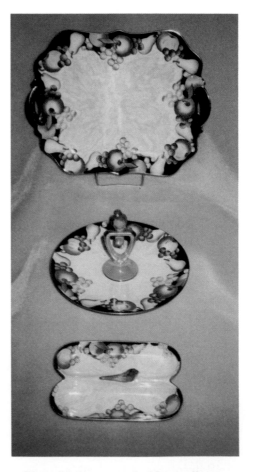

*Photo #4. Items matched by a collector.*

40

Photo #5. Matching plate and vase.

Photo #6. A collection of wall pockets.

Photo #8. Figural painted differently from that displayed in photo #9.

Photo #7. An over abundance of Noritake pieces.

Photo #9. Figural – mold as same as photo #8.

Photo #11. Salt set.

Photo #12. Individual salts.

Photo #10. Figural showing queue down the back.

Photo #13. Individual salts.

Photo #14. Individual salt.

*Photo #15. Original lithograph by Homer Conant.*

*Photo #17. Close-up of lithograph.*

*Photo #16. Noritake, design copied from Homer Conant lithograph.*

*Photo #18. Noritake plate, design is an adaptation from an early 1920 lithograph.*

*Photo #20. Cardboard container for piquante face powder by Bolgate and Co. of N.Y.*

*Photo #19. Noritake tray, design is an adaption from an early 1920 lithograph.*

## Noritake Sets and Contents

Many different types of sets are available to collectors and listed below are ones they may find in their travels. Much of this information was gleaned from old catalog ads. Each of these "sets" may include some or all the items listed next to it.

After dinner coffee set – also called a demitasse set, consists of a tall pot with a long spout, cups, saucers, and sometimes a tray and a creamer and sugar bowl.

Asparagus set – (decorated with an asparagus motif), consists of a master dish and smaller serving dishes.

Berry set – made up of a larger perforated bowl and underplate and small individual bowls.

Berry sugar and cream set – consists of a sugar shaker and matching creamer.

Beverage set – consists of a covered beverage container and matching creamer.

Bread and butter set – consists of a larger dish (approximately 7½" wide) and smaller butter pats about 3½" wide.

Breakfast set – adult size can be made up of an individual size coffee pot, individual chocolate pot, egg cup, pancake server, breakfast plate, cup and saucer, creamer and sugar bowl, salt and pepper; child's size, also called an oatmeal set, consists of a bowl, pitcher, and plate.

Bridge set – made up of a set of four ashtrays and sometimes a matching tray and cigarette holder.

Cake set – consists of a larger serving dish and smaller matching plates.

Celery set – made up of a larger serving dish and individual salts.

Cheese and cracker set – round attached underplate containing a small bowl in center with a cover. It will also have a perforated insert which is placed inside on top of ice chips to keep the cheese cold.

Chip and dip set – similar to the cheese and cracker set but does not have perforated insert.

Chocolate set – consists of a tall pot with a short spout, cups, saucers, and sometimes a tray.

Cider set – consists of a bulbous shaped pitcher and matching tumblers, also called a lemonade set.

Coaster set – made up of six to eight individual coasters.

Condiment set – consists of a mustard pot, salt and pepper shakers, toothpick holder, and tray.

Console set – also called a mantle set, consists of a bowl, and often a pair of candlesticks and vases or urn or two side urns.

Cordial set – also called a liquor or decanter set, made up of a decanter, pedestalled glasses, and often has a matching tray.

Corn set – (decorated with ears of corn), consists of a master dish and smaller serving dishes just big enough for an ear of corn.

Creamer and sugar set – consists of a sugar bowl and a creamer.

Cruet set – also called an oil and vinegar set, has oil and vinegar containers and sometimes has a salt and pepper and matching tray.

Decanter set – also called a liquor or cordial set, made up of a decanter and pedestalled glasses and often has a matching tray.

Demitasse set – also called an after dinner coffee set, consists of a pot, cups, saucers, and sometimes a matching tray and creamer and sugar bowl.

Desk set – made up of a tray, letter holder, stamp box, ink blotter, calendar holder, inkwell with insert, and blotter corners.

Dessert set – consists of several individual plates that have an indentation for a cup, each plate comes with a cup, also called snack set, sandwich set, refreshment set, or toast set.

Dinner set – can consist of many pieces, dinner plates, breakfast plates, tea plates, pie plates, bread and butter plates, salad plates, cream soup bowls, bouillon cups and saucers, fruit saucers, cups and saucers, after dinner cups and saucers, oatmeal dishes, small platter, medium platter, large platter, sugar bowl and cream pitcher, pickle dish, sauce or gravy boat, covered casserole or baker, covered serving dish, open vegetable dish, cake plate, salad bowl, teapot, covered butter dish, coasters, celery dish, and individual salts. There is also a child's play dinner set made up of a serving platter, covered casserole, dinner plates, cups and saucers, covered teapot, and sugar bowl and creamer.

Dresser set – can consist of a tray, hatpin holder, cologne bottle, pin dish, perfume bottle, trinket dish or box, stickpin holder, powder box, hair receiver, ring tree, hatpin holder, and sometimes a pair of candlesticks.

Fish set – consists of a large platter and small individual size dishes, some are even found in the shape of a fish.

Fruit set – consists of a tray, pedestalled bowl and individual pedestalled small bowls, similar to a punch set but smaller in size.

Game set – made up of a large serving platter and smaller serving dishes, decorated with scenes of wild game.

Hostess set – also called a sweetmeat set, consists of a covered lacquer box and contains several individual dishes that fit inside.

Ice cream set – consists of a main serving dish and smaller bowls or plates, generally the tray is oblong and the plates are square in shape.

Lemonade set – made up of a bulbous shaped pitcher and matching tumblers, also called a cider set.

Liquor set – also called a cordial or decanter set, made up

of a decanter and pedestalled glasses and often has a matching tray.

Lobster set – two-piece item made up of a bowl and underplate decorated with paintings of lobsters.

Luncheon set – similar to a dinner set but does not have dinner plates but a smaller luncheon plate, also does not contain all of the items in a complete dinner set.

Mantle set – also called a console set, consists of a bowl, and often a pair of candlesticks and vases or urn or two side urns.

Mayonnaise set – consists of a bowl, underplate and matching ladle, also called a whip cream set.

Milk set – contains a milk pitcher and matching tumblers.

Nut set – consists of a medium size bowl and smaller ones to hold nuts, some sets are even decorated with a nut motif.

Oatmeal set – also called a child's breakfast set, consists of a bowl, pitcher, and plate.

Oil and vinegar set – also called a cruet set, has oil and vinegar containers and sometimes a salt and pepper and matching tray.

Open salt and pepper set – consists of a tray, pepper shaker, and open salt dish.

Punch bowl set – consists of a punch bowl which is often pedestalled and two pieces, and matching cups.

Refreshment set – also called a dessert or snack set, or sandwich or toast set, consists of several individual plates that have an indentation for a cup, each plate comes with a matching cup.

Relish set – consists of a main serving dish, smaller than a celery dish and individual salts.

Salad set – consists of a large bowl and smaller matching bowls or plates, some even come with porcelain serving utensils, a long handled fork and spoon.

Salt and pepper set – made up of a salt shaker or open salt and pepper shaker.

Sandwich set – also called a refreshment or snack set, or a toast or dessert set, it's a two-piece item consisting of a cup and matching plate that has an indentation for holding the cup.

Seasoning set – made up of a tray, oil and vinegar cruets, salt and pepper shakers, and a mustard pot.

Sherbet set – sometimes comes with a tray, consists of a set of metal holders which hold small porcelain bowls for sherbet.

Smoke set – consists of a tray, ashtray, humidor, tobacco jar, match holder, and cigarette holder.

Snack set – also called a dessert or refreshment set, or sandwich or toast set, it's a two-piece item consisting of a cup and matching plate that has an indentation for holding the cup.

Stacked tea set – made up of a teapot, tea tile, creamer and sugar bowl which stack up on top of one another.

Sweetmeat set – also called a hostess set, consists of a covered lacquer box which contains several individual dishes that fit inside.

Tankard set – consists of a tankard and matching mugs or steins.

Tea set – adult size contains teapot, cups, saucers, sugar bowl, creamer, and sometimes a matching tray. Children's play size and doll size can have same items.

Tete-a-tete set – made up of a teapot, sugar bowl, creamer, two cups and saucers.

Toast set – also called a dessert or refreshment set, or sandwich or snack set, it's a two-piece item consisting of a cup and matching plate that has an indentation for holding that cup.

Vanity set – consists of two perfume bottles and a powder box.

Whip cream set – also called a mayonnaise set, made up of a small bowl, matching underplate and serving ladle.

## Some rules for collectors to follow:

Don't invest money you can't spare but do buy the best you can afford.

Don't be a slave to fads – what's "hot" today may not be tomorrow. Collect your items because you love them. The only certain thing about the future is that we cannot predict what will happen.

Don't buy parts of sets and hope to fill in. Sometimes a collector does find that missing piece but it can take years of searching. It does happen but it's the exception not the rule. If you do buy incomplete sets – don't pay a premium price.

Knowledge is power. It's been said "What a person doesn't know can't hurt him" but in collectible market it can often be "what a person doesn't know CAN hurt him." Study your books and study your pieces. Talk with other collectors and dealers. Go to as many antique shows as you can. Be an informed buyer.

Collectors should cultivate dealers – after a while they will know what you like and call you or send a photo of an available item. They can in essence become your "picker."

Keep good records of your items. Take photographs and/or videos. But do not keep these in the same house with the items! List your pieces along with their backstamp, where acquired and date and the cost and condition. Catalog your whole collection. Even if you never have a robbery or fire you can always use this information when and if you want to sell some of the items.

Check over the items being purchased carefully. Cracks, chips, hairlines, repairs, and worn gold should be avoided. If pieces do have these flaws make sure the price reflects the damage.

Teacup & Saucer

Chocolate Cup &
Saucer

After-Dinner
Coffee Cup & Saucer

Both May Have Cover

2 - Handled
Bouillon Cup
& Saucer

Handleless
Bouillon Cup
& Saucer

Tea Strainer
With Bottom

Teapots, Shorter In Height
Have Long Spouts, Always Have Covers

Black Coffee Pot
Tall With Long Spout
Always Has Cover

Milk Pitchers, Generally Medium In
Height, Short Spout, Some Have Covers

Chocolate Pot
Tall With Short Spout
Always Has Cover

Profiles of some of the different shapes of pots and cups found. Many a novice collector doesn't know the difference between a chocolate and a coffee pot, how to tell a demitasse cup from a chocolate cup, etc. A chocolate pot is distinguished from a coffee pot by its short spout, a bouillon cup is either two-handled or handleless, some bouillon cups even have covers. The after-dinner coffee cup or demitasse is the smallest of all, the chocolate cup is tall and narrow. Many of the cups have a pedestal shaped base.

# Backstamps

The majority of the backstamps shown are actual photographs that the Noritake Company has supplied or that I was able to obtain from my items. The others are hand drawn facsimiles of marks submitted by the company or collectors who have tried to help us in our quest for knowledge.

The Noritake Company did not realize how important the dating of these pieces would be to collectors in later years and regretfully they do not have information regarding many of their marks. They are not sure of many cut-off dates or when one mark started and another was discontinued. They believe the letter M appeared in their backstamps until the letter N was registered in 1953. The American occupation of Japan lasted until 1952 when "Occupied Japan" should also have been placed on the wares. In 1953 they started using the N.

According to the Noritake Company, the designs and shapes of most of their wares were European preferred and were for the Western taste. They assume that their old marks have the English backstamps on them even for the domestic market in Japan because they never possessed a Japanese written backstamp until about fifteen years ago when they started manufacturing authentic Japanese wares. In Japan, many manufacturers adopted the English spelling of brand names for their commodity even for the domestic market.

The Noritake Company does not know nor can they guess how the pattern numbers were assigned. These are found in many of the backstamps.

The company was only required to have the country of origin on their items and naturally added their own logo as they were very proud of the wares they had produced. I have tried to date the pieces as carefully as possible with the company's help and also relying upon old catalogs and brochures.

Most of the information regarding the dating of backstamps has been gathered at a slow pace and at times it has almost been like pulling teeth. Some was gleaned from the old catalogs, some from collectors, some from my own collection, and the majority from the Noritake Company. In many cases we can date the beginning year of manufacture for items with a particular backstamp but not when it ended. Obviously anything with "Nippon" printed in the backstamp as country of origin dates back to an earlier period and those with "Occupied Japan" date after World War II until 1952. Marks having an N in them date from 1953 on. Some marks can only be guessed at as to the time period. New information is surfacing all the time and I am sure there will be many corrections and additions made to this listing over the years but as it now stands is a guideline and the best that we have available. I have tried to be as accurate as possible and only wish it were a more complete list. Hopefully future researchers and historians may be able to elaborate on this information.

**Morimura Brothers Era, 1878–1884.** There are records that during this period Morimura Brothers had their own decoration kiln in Japan but what backstamp they used is unknown.

**1884–1890.** In 1882, Morimura Brothers changed their business nature to wholesaling from retailing and had dozens of their affiliated decoration factories all over Japan. **Backstamps #1 through #4** are from that era. The country of origin was marked in Chinese characters on these, not in English. In 1890 the McKinley Tariff Act was passed and beginning in 1891 it became necessary that all the products coming to the United States be stamped. Since that time "Nippon" had appeared as part of the backstamp until "Japan" replaced it in 1921.

**Backstamp #5** was registered in Japan in 1919 but the items bearing this backstamp can date back as far as 1891. If the backstamp is green it's an indication of first grade wares, the blue backstamp means second grade.

In 1904, the Noritake factory was founded and called Nippon Kaisha Ltd. (now, Noritake Co., Limited). The company was established at 510 Mukai, Takahamura, Aichi Gun, Aichi Prefecture. "Noritake" took its name from the village of Noritake. The Noritake Company says in their brochure entitled "History of the Noritake Backstamp" that

> "the trademark which is found on manufactured goods can be called a kind of face of the enterprise which serves society as a guarantee of the quality of the goods, and expresses the responsibility and reliability of the company. Trademarks or brand names which were put on various kinds of porcelain represented the spirit of our founders who pioneered in the manufacture of chinaware. They also symbolized Japanese porcelain which has spread to every part of the world. The trademark of a product is the primary means by which the manufacturer wins the respect of the consumers for the quality and reliability of its products."

**Backstamp #6** was registered in Japan in 1908. The RC stands for Royal Crockery (fine china). The symbol design is called "Yajirobe" (toy of balance). It symbolizes the balance in management.

**Backstamp #7** is found on items manufactured for the domestic market in Japan. Items bearing this mark date back as early as 1906. The date of registration, however, is unknown. It has the RC for Royal Crockery (fine china) and the symbol design "Yajirobe."

**Backstamp #8** was registered in Japan in 1911 although the year of manufacture of items bearing this mark is as early as 1906. The RC stands for Royal Crockery (fine china). Pieces with this backstamp were intended for the domestic market in Japan.

**Backstamp #9** is found on items intended for the domestic market in Japan. The RC stands for Royal Crockery (fine china). 1906 is the year they started to use this backstamp and it was registered in Japan in 1911.

**Backstamp #10** was used on items being exported to the United States. The first year of manufacture was 1906. The mark was registered both in Japan and the United States in 1911. The RC stands for Royal Crockery (fine china).

**Backstamp #11** was used on items intended for export to the United States. The earliest year of manufacture was 1906 but the date of registration is unknown. The centered design of the stamp was taken from the Chinese character "Komaru" meaning difficulty. In the export business, the Noritake Company had to deal with people from foreign lands who thought and acted in a manner somewhat different from which they were accustomed. Since they had to overcome these difficulties, they chose this character and drew a new design. This progressive thinking was representative of the people of the Meiji Era.

**Backstamp #12** is most likely a Noritake backstamp although the company cannot be 100% sure. They feel strongly that it appears to be Noritake's. They say that there were wide ranges of the stylization of the character "Komaru" and this is most likely one of them. The backstamp was probably used on items intended for export beginning in 1906–1908.

**Backstamp #13** is a variation of #12 and found on pieces in the white and gold pattern. It evidently does not date back further than 1912.*

**Backstamp #14** was used on items being exported to the United States. The beginning year of manufacture was 1906 but the registration date is unknown.

**Backstamp #15** was used on items intended for export to the United States. The year of manufacture began in 1906 but the registration date is unknown.

**Backstamp #16** was used on items being exported to the United Kingdom. It was registered in London in 1908 and in 1911 in Japan. Manufacturing began in 1908. The sign of the "komaru" is used, see backstamp #12.

**Backstamp #17** is a variation of #16 but includes design number.

**Backstamp #18** is similar to #16 and was evidently used on items being exported out of Japan. It probably falls into the same time period.

**Backstamp #19** was used on items intended for export to the United States. The year of manufacture began in 1906 and it was registered in Japan in 1911. RC stands for Royal Crockery (fine china).

**Backstamp #20** was registered in London in 1908 and manufacture also began the same year. The "komaru" sign is also incorporated into this backstamp, see backstamp #11.

**Backstamp #21** was used on items intended for export to the United States. The "M" stands for Morimura and the wreath was designed from the crest of the Morimuras. Manufacturing items with this backstamp began in 1911. This mark was registered both in Japan and the United States in 1911.

**Backstamp #22** has the M in the middle which stands for Morimura and the wreath was designed from the crest of the Morimuras. Manufacturing of items with this backstamp began in 1912 but the registration date is unknown.

**Backstamp #23** is a variation of #22 but indicates that the piece has been hand painted.

**Backstamp #24** is another variation of #22 and also indicates that this piece was handpainted and in 'The Vitry" pattern.

**Backstamp #25** is again another variation of #22 and indicates that the piece was handpainted and in the "Sedan" pattern. This particular mark was used on the first dinnerware set manufactured by the Noritake factory in 1914. The registration date is unknown but the pattern number is listed as D1441.

**Backstamp #26** is the backstamp used on items sent to India and Southeast Asia. RC stands for Royal Crockery (fine china). The year of manufacture began in 1914 but the mark was not registered in India until 1926. This was the first time that laurel leaves were used with the RC mark.

**Backstamp #27** bears the letter M which stands for the Morimuras. The Noritake Company says that the country of origin "Nippon" was changed in this mark to "Made in Japan" as early as 1918, however, they have no record to show the date it was registered. The Noritake Company cannot trace whether or not the green ink is older.

**Backstamp #28** is a variation of #27 but has the words "US Design Pat. Applied For" added to it.

**Backstamp #29** is again a variation of #27 but utilizes Japanese characters in its backstamp.

**Backstamp #30** is another variation of #27 but also gives us the pattern which is "The Vitry," plus Japanese characters and the number "13672."

**Backstamp #31** is another variation of #27 but this mark is found on the white and gold pattern items and gives the early pattern number "16034."

**Backstamp #32** is a variation of #27 giving us Japanese characters and the "No. 25920."

**Backstamp #33** is another variation of #27 giving us Japanese characters plus "No. 29612."

**Backstamp #34** is a variation of #27 giving us more Japanese characters plus "#39556."

**Backstamp #35** is again another variation of #27 but it is the mark familiar to collectors as that of being on the white and gold pattern items. It bears Japanese characters and the pattern number of "43061."

**Backstamp #36** is another variation of #27 and gives us the pattern name "Amesbury" plus the "US Design Pat. 61231."

**Backstamp #37** is a version of #27 but is familiar to collectors as one of the marks found on the Azalea pattern. It includes Japanese characters plus "19322."

**Backstamp #38** is similar to #27 but does not include the words "hand painted."

**Backstamp #39** is a variation of #38 but also includes the words "US Design Pat. 61235."

**Backstamp #40** is a version of #38 but includes the pattern name of "Sheridan."

**Backstamp #41** is also a version of #38 and includes the pattern name of "Lancashire" plus the words "US Design Pat. Applied For."

**Backstamp #42** is a version of #38 and includes the pattern name of "Daventry" plus "US Design Pat. Applied For."

**Backstamp #43** is still another version of #38 and includes the pattern name of "Amarillo" plus "US Design Pat. Applied For."

**Backstamp #44** is again another version of #38 and is familiar to collectors as that of the one found on the Modjeska pattern items.

**Backstamp #45** is a version of #38 but is the one found on items in the Grasmere pattern, also see Mark #64.

**Backstamp #46** is a version of #38 and found with the pattern name of "Roseara" and the words "US Design Pat. Applied For."

**Backstamp #47** is a version of #38 and is found on items in the Winona pattern.

**Backstamp #48** is a version of #38 and lists the pattern name of Floreal and the words "US Design Patent Applied For."

**Backstamp #49** is a version of #38 and is found on pieces decorated with the Howo bird. It bears the number 10733.*

**Backstamp #50** is a version of #27 but the words "Made in Japan" have been changed to "Japan."

**Backstamp #51** is a version of #50 but the pattern name of "Goldcroft" has been included.

**Backstamp #52** is a version of #50 except that the words "hand painted" do not appear.

**Backstamp #53** is a variation of mark #12 but has the words "Made in Japan" included. Note the "komaru" sign which is incorporated into the backstamp.

**Backstamp #54** is a variation of #53 but no longer says "Nippon" and includes the pattern number found on the white and gold pieces, "No. 16034."

**Backstamp #55** is found on items decorated in the Noritake Howo pattern but the company does not know when the mark was first used or when it was discontinued.

**Backstamp #56** is a mark which the company does not know when it was first used or ended, however, this same backstamp appears on other dinner sets all collected from Australia.

**Backstamp #57** is found on pieces in the white and gold pattern. Pattern #D175 has been in production since 1912 and it remains a popular pattern all over the world even now. This mark was registered in Japan in 1930 and in the United States in 1950.

**Backstamp #58** is a variation of #57 but also includes Japanese characters.

**Backstamp #59** was registered in Japan in 1931. The "M" stands for the Morimuras.

**Backstamp #60** is a version of #59 but included the pattern name of "Irvington."

**Backstamp #61** is a version of #59 but includes the pattern name of "Eltovar" and the words "US Design Pat."

**Backstamp #62** is a version of #59 and includes the pattern names of "Ashby" plus the words "US Design Pat. Applied For."

**Backstamp #63** is a backstamp for which the company has no information as to when it began and when it ended. It does have the "M" standing for Morimuras in the mark so it has to date before 1953.

**Backstamp #64** is a variation of #63 but gives the pattern name of "Grasmere" plus the words "US Design Pat. 76567." The Grasmere items also are found backstamped with #45.

**Backstamp #65** bears the "M" standing for the Morimuras. It was registered in Japan in 1933. The familiar M in wreath mark was changed to show laurel leaves with a ribbon on the bottom. This is the basic design of the backstamp used today only the letter N is used.

**Backstamp #66** is a version of #65 and found on the Linden pattern items.

**Backstamp #67** is also a version of #65 and found on the Linden items but also gives the "US Design Pat. 98217."

**Backstamp #68** is a version of #65 and found on items in the Belvoir pattern.

**Backstamp #69** is a version of #65 and found on pieces bearing the Berenda pattern, "124632."

**Backstamp #70** is also a version of #65 and found on items in the Homeric pattern.

**Backstamp #71** is a version of #65 and found on Lynbrook pattern items.

**Backstamp #72** is a version of #65 but the words have been changed to "Made in Japan."

**Backstamp #73** has the "M" standing for the Morimuras. This mark was registered in Japan in 1933.

**Backstamp #74** is a version of #73 but has the words "US Design Pat. Applied For."

**Backstamp #75** is a mark familiar to Azalea pattern collectors. This mark was registered in Japan in 1934.

**Backstamp #76** is another mark found on the Azalea pieces but has the numbers "252622" added. These items were given as premiums by the Larkin Company of Buffalo, New York.

**Backstamp #77** was registered in Japan in 1934.

**Backstamp #78** bears the "M" for the Morimuras and was registered in 1940.

**Backstamp #79** bears the "M" for the Morimuras and is similar to #78 except for the difference in the crown on top.

**Backstamp #80** was registered in Japan in 1940. The "komaru" symbol meaning difficulty was incorporated in it. See backstamp #11 for further information about "komaru." Some have referred to this mark as a "spider" but the company indicates that this is false information.

**Backstamp #81** was registered in Japan in 1940 and bears the "M" for the Morimuras.

**Backstamp #82** was registered in Japan in 1940 and bears the "komaru" mark, see #11. The initials NTK stand for Nippon Toki Kaisha.

**Backstamp #83** was registered in Japan in 1941.

**Backstamp #84** is that of "Rose China." Immediately after the war the company resumed production of china but for various reasons they could not manufacture the same high-quality china that they had made and exported earlier. Since they wanted to keep the Noritake mark for only the highest quality products they temporarily used the Rose China backstamp. Manufacture of these pieces began in 1946 and the mark was registered in Japan in 1950.

**Backstamp #85** was registered in Japan in 1949.

**Backstamp #86** is a variation of #85.

**Backstamp #87** was registered in Japan in 1949 and the United States in 1950. Manufacture of these items began in 1947. This mark was only used for a year and a half and items bearing this backstamp should have been marked "Rose China." The "komaru" symbol is used, see #11. This mark reflects the conditions of the country during the years of the occupation.

**Backstamp #88** is a variation of #87.

**Backstamp #89** is also variation of #87.

**Backstamp #90** was registered in Japan in 1949.

**Backstamp #91** was registered in Japan in 1949. The year of manufacture also began this year. The "M" stands for the Morimuras.

**Backstamps #92** was registered in the United States in 1950. Because Noritake is the name of a place, the word could not be officially registered as a trademark. However, because of the consistently high quality of their products, they were finally given permission to register their name.

**Backstamp #93** was registered in Japan in 1953 and was the first backstamp used with the letter "N."

**Backstamp #94** is the current backstamp and was registered in Japan in 1964. N is taken from their formal name Nippon Toki.

**Backstamp #95** is a variation of #94.

**Backstamp #96** was evidently used in 1953 or later it bears the "N."

**Backstamp #97** is a version of #57 and #58 and is found on today's white and gold dishes.

**Backstamp #98** is a variation of #50 but has words "Japanese Design Patent Applied For," added.

**Backstamp #99** is a variation of mark #27.

*Japanese characters drawn are fictitious.

Backstamp #1

Backstamp #5

Backstamp #2

Backstamp #6

Backstamp #3

Backstamp #7

Backstamp #4

Backstamp #8

Backstamp #9

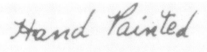

Backstamp #13

Backstamp #10

Backstamp #14

Backstamp #11

Backstamp #15

Backstamp #12

Backstamp #16

53

Backstamp #17

Backstamp #21

Backstamp #18

Backstamp #22

Backstamp #19

Backstamp #23

Backstamp #20

Backstamp #24

Backstamp #25

Backstamp #26

Backstamp #27

Backstamp #28

Backstamp #29

Backstamp #30

Backstamp #31

Backstamp #32

Backstamp #33

Backstamp #34

Backstamp #35

Backstamp #36

Backstamp #37

Backstamp #38

Backstamp #39

Backstamp #40

Backstamp #41

Backstamp #42

Backstamp #43

Backstamp #44

Backstamp #45

Backstamp #49

Backstamp #53

Backstamp #46

Backstamp #50

Backstamp #54

Backstamp #47

Backstamp #51

Backstamp #55

Backstamp #48

Backstamp #52

Backstamp #56

Backstamp #57

Backstamp #61

Backstamp #65

Backstamp #58

Backstamp #62

Backstamp #66

Backstamp #59

Backstamp #63

Backstamp #67

Backstamp #60

Backstamp #64

Backstamp #68

Backstamp #69

Backstamp #73

Backstamp #77

Backstamp #70

Backstamp #74

Backstamp #78

Backstamp #71

Backstamp #75

Backstamp #79

Backstamp #72

Backstamp #76

Backstamp #80

Backstamp #81

Backstamp #82

Backstamp #83

Backstamp #84

Backstamp #85

Backstamp #86

Backstamp #87

Backstamp #88

Backstamp #89

Backstamp #90

Backstamp #91

Noritaké

Backstamp #92

Backstamp #93

Backstamp #95

Backstamp #94

Backstamp #96

Backstamp #97

Backstamp #98

Backstamp #99

# Pricing Information

Price quotes listed are for similar pieces in MINT condition. Adjustments in price should be made for cracks, chips, worn gold, repairs, etc. Prices will vary from dealer to dealer and also in different localities. Be sure to check over each item carefully before purchase.

In this guide you will find estimated collector's RETAIL prices listed. These prices do not mean that an item is worth exactly what is printed, they are merely a guide to assist both collectors and dealers. Use them only as a starting point.

Well-executed pieces are always in demand and their prices continue to rise each year. The increased sophistication and knowledge on the part of today's collector has driven up the prices of the really fine pieces. Because of this, some of the more common run-of-the-mill items have not risen at all in value and may even have dropped in price. Small nut dishes, poorly decorated dinnerware items and similar wares will always be flea market material.

There are always collecting trends and the Noritake field is no exception. Art Deco style pieces seem to have captured the fancy of many collectors and the prices realized for these items reflect it. The patterns are often geometric cubist designs, stylized flowers, butterflies, and birds. Flappers and elegantly dressed ladies are a favorite. Iridescent finishes and luster glazes were frequently used as well as a number of bold color combinations. Art Deco is definitely "in" and making its presence known.

Collectors should look for Noritake pieces having good workmanship, handpainted decoration, mint or near mint condition, and overall quality. Collectors should also buy items that personally appeal to them regardless of what the collecting trends are at the moment.

One must also realize that the Noritake books are not like mail order catalogs where you can simply call in your order and say "I'll take two of plate #43 and one of #87." Each dealer has to hunt diligently for his items. He has to attend auctions, shows, flea markets, estate sales, etc., and all this is reflected in his prices. If he got a good bargain he will often pass it on, if not, then the price will be steeper. Everyone likes to buy at low prices and sell at high ones. In fact, inflation is often described as when the prices you get look good but the prices you pay look awful. Make worthy choices and avoid taking foolish chances.

# Photos and Descriptions

Plates 1 thru 447 are featured in
*The Collector's Encyclopedia of Noritake*, First Series.

*Plate 448. Figural covered box, 10¼" tall, green mark
#27. $1200.00–1300.00.*

*Plate 449. Figural covered box, 6½" tall, red mark #27.
$300.00–400.00.*

*Plate 448A. Same as 448.*

Plate 450. Figural covered box, 8" tall, red mark #27.
$1300.00–1500.00.

Plate 451. Figural covered box, 8" tall, red mark #27.
$1300.00–1500.00.

Plate 452. Figurine, 7" tall, green
mark #27. $450.00–550.00.

Plate 453. Figural clown box, 5½" tall,
green mark #27. $275.00–295.00.

Plate 454. Figural lamp, 9" tall,
green mark #32. $1100.00–1200.00.

Plate 455. Figural lamp, 9¾" tall, green mark #27. $950.00–1100.00.

Plate 456. Figural lamp, 9¾" tall, green mark #27. $950.00–1100.00.

Plate 457. Figural dresser dolls, 6" tall, green mark #32. $275.00–295.00 each.

Plate 458. Figural dresser doll, 6¼" tall, red mark #27. $285.00–310.00.

Plate 459. Figurines, 7" tall and 6½" tall, lady has removable pierced lid, green mark #27. Left, $500.00–550.00; right, $550.00–600.00.

Plate 460. Figural dresser doll, 6" tall, red mark #27. $275.00–295.00.

Plate 461. Figural dresser doll, 6" tall, red mark #27. $275.00–295.00.

Plate 462. Figural lamp, 8" tall, similar to Royal Doulton "Polly Peacham," green mark #27. $900.00–1050.00.

Plate 463. Figural dresser doll, 7" tall, red mark #27. $300.00–325.00.

Plate 464. Figural dresser doll, 7" tall, red mark #27. $300.00–325.00.

Left: Plate 465. Figural dresser doll/talcum powder shaker, 6" tall, red mark #27. $275.00–295.00.

Right: Plate 466. Figural dresser doll, 5½" tall, green mark #32. $275.00–295.00.

Plate 468. *Figural dresser dolls, 9" tall, green #27, 4" tall, red mark #27. Left, $395.00–425.00; right, 175.00–195.00.*

Plate 467. *Figural dresser dolls, 5½" tall, green mark #32; 5" tall, green mark #32. $275.00–295.00 each.*

Plate 469. *Figural dresser doll, 6½" tall, red mark #27. $400.00–450.00.*

Plate 470. *Figural dresser doll, 6" tall, green mark #27. $285.00–310.00.*

Pate 471. Figural dresser doll, 6" tall, green mark #32.
$275.00–295.00.

Plate 472. Figural dresser doll, 6" tall, green mark #32.
$275.00–295.00.

Plate 473. Figural dresser dolls, 8½" tall, red mark
#27. $395.00–425.00.

Plate 474. Figural powder box, 4¾" tall, green
mark #32. $300.00–350.00.

*Plate 475. Figural dresser dolls, 5¾" tall, green mark #32. $275.00–295.00 each.*

*Plate 476. Figural powder box, 5¾" tall, green #27. $275.00–295.00.*

*Plate 477. Figural dresser set: doll, 6½" tall, green mark #27. Tray, 11" long. $375.00–410.00.*

Plate 478. Figural dreser set: tray is 7½" long, doll is 6" tall, green mark #27. $375.00–410.00.

Plate 479. Figural powder box, 5" tall, red mark #27. $275.00–295.00.

Plate 480. Figural powder box, green mark #27. $275.00–295.00.

Plate 481. Figural dresser set: doll is 6" tall, tray is 10¼" long, red mark #27. $395.00–425.00.

Plate 482. Figural dresser doll, 5½" tall, red mark #27. $285.00–310.00.

Plate 483. Figural dresser doll, 5¾" tall, green mark #27. $275.00–295.00.

Plate 484. Figural dresser set: tray is 12½" long, green mark #27. $400.00–430.00.

Pate 485. Figural powder puff and box, 4" wide, green
mark #27. $295.00–310.00.

Plate 486. Figural pin dish, 5" wide, red mark #27.
$275.00–295.00.

Plate 487. Figural pin dishes, 2¾" wide, red mark #27. $40.00–60.00.

Plate 488. Figural powder puff and box, 4"
wide, red mark #27. $295.00–310.00.

Plate 488A. Same as plate 488.
$295.00–310.00.

Plate 489. Figural pin dish, 4¼" wide,
green mark #27. $275.00–295.00.

Plate 490. Figural powder box,
3½" tall, green mark #27.
$70.00–90.00.

Plate 491. Figural pin dish, 4" long, red mark #27. $295.00–310.00.

Plate 492. Figural pin dish, 4" long, red mark #27. $295.00–310.00.

Plate 493. Figural inkwell, 4" tall, red mark #27. $275.00–295.00.

Plate 494. Figural inkwell, 4½" tall, green mark #27. $275.00–295.00.

Plate 495. Figural cosmetic jar, 3" tall, red mark #27. $275.00–295.00.

Plate 496. Figural cosmetic jar, 4" tall, red mark #27. $100.00–150.00.

Plate 497. Figural inkwell, 3" tall, red mark #27. $110.00–125.00.

Plate 498. Figural powder puff box, 4" wide, red mark #27. $150.00–195.00.

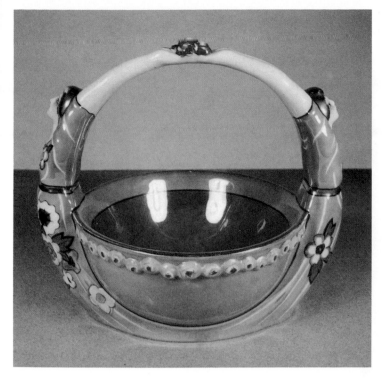

*Plate 499. Figural bowl, 6" tall, red mark #27. $1200.00–1300.00.*

*Plate 499A. Figural bowl, 6" tall, red mark #27 – front view of #499. $1200.00–1300.00.*

*Plate 500. Figural bowl, 6" tall, red mark #27. $1200.00–1300.00.*

Plate 501. Figural bowl, 6" tall, red mark #27. $1200.00–1300.00.

Plate 502. Figural bowl, 5" long, red mark #27. $75.00–90.00.

Plate 503. Figural bowl, 5½" wide, red mark #27. $1200.00–1300.00.

Plate 504. Figural inkwell, 4½" tall, red mark #27. $275.00–310.00.

Plate 506. Figural dish, 6½" long, green mark #27. $200.00–225.00.

Plate 505. Figural bowl, 9" wide, red mark #27. $275.00–310.00.

Plate 507. Figural basket, 5" tall, red mark #27. $65.00–80.00.

Plate 508. Figural bowl, 6" wide, green mark #27. $215.00–240.00.

Plate 509. Figural dish, 5¾" wide, red mark #27. $75.00–95.00.

Plate 510. Figural bowl, 9" wide, red mark #27. $325.00–350.00.

Plate 511. Figural bowl, 6" wide, red mark #27. $275.00–295.00.

Photo 512. Figural dish, 7½" long, green mark #27. $115.00–135.00.

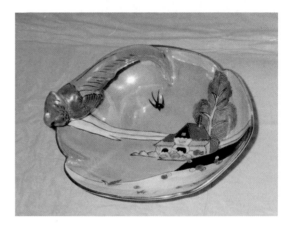

Plate 513. Figural bowl, 6½" wide, red mark #27. $65.00–80.00.

Plate 514. Figural bowl, red mark #27. $95.00–110.00.

Plate 516. Figural dish, 8½" long, red mark #27. $115.00–130.00.

Plate 515. Figural dish, 7½" long, green mark #27. $115.00–130.00.

Plate 518. Figural bowl, 7" wide, red mark #27. $135.00–150.00.

Plate 517. Figural bowl, 7" wide, red mark #27. $135.00–150.00.

Plate 519. Figural dish, 5½" wide, red mark #27. $95.00–110.00.

Plate 520. Figural dish, 5½" wide, red mark #27. $95.00–110.00.

Plate 521. Figural dish, 5½" wide, green mark #27. $150.00–175.00.

Plate 522. Figural bowl, 7½" wide, green mark #27. $115.00–130.00.

Plate 523. Figural flower frogs, 3½" tall, red mark #27. $250.00–300.00 each.

Plate 524. Combination bowl and figural flower frog bowl, 5" wide, green mark #27. $325.00–375.00.

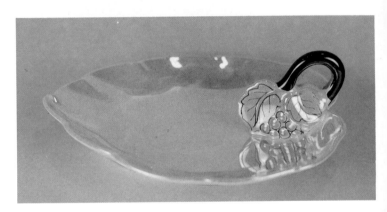

Plate 525. Figural nappy, 7½" long, green mark #27. $75.00–85.00.

Plate 526. Figural flower frog, 3½" tall, red mark #27. $135.00–160.00.

Plate 527. Figural frog, 4½" tall, red mark #27. $225.00–250.00.

Plate 528. Figural bowl, 6½" wide, red mark #27. $75.00–85.00.

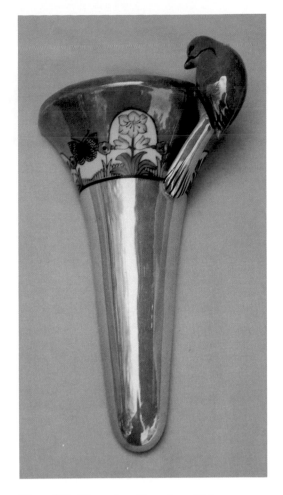

Plate 529. Figural wall pocket, 8" long, green mark #27. $175.00–195.00.

Plate 530. Figural bowl, 6½" wide, red mark #27. $75.00–85.00.

Plate 531. Figural candy dish, 7½" wide, red mark #27. $200.00–250.00.

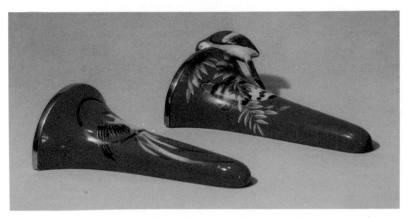

Plate 532. Figural wall pockets, 8" long, red mark #27, green mark #27. Left, $150.00–175.00; right, $175.00–195.00.

Plate 533. Figural ashtray, 4" wide, green mark #27. $170.00–190.00.

Plate 534. Figural ashtray, 2¾" wide, red mark #27. $150.00–175.00.

Plate 535. Figural ashtray, 2¾" wide, green mark #27. $170.00–190.00.

Plate 536. Figural ashtray, 3" tall, green mark #27. $125.00–150.00.

Plate 537. Figural ashtrays, 2¾" wide, red mark #27. $225.00–250.00 each.

Plate 538. Figural ashtray, 3½" wide, green mark #27. $190.00–225.00.

Plate 539. Figural ashtray, 4" tall, green mark #27. $300.00–325.00.

Plate 540. Figural ashtray, 4" tall, green mark #27. $300.00–325.00.

Plate 541. Figural ashtray, 6" wide, green mark #27. $325.00–350.00.

Plate 544, Figural ashtray, 2½" tall, green mark #27. $75.00–85.00.

Plate 542. Figural ashtray, 4" tall, green mark #27. $300.00–325.00.

Plate 543. Figural ashtray, 3½" diameter, red mark #27. $65.00–75.00.

Plate 545. Figural ashtray, 5" wide, red mark #27. $275.00–295.00.

Plate 546. Figural ashtray, 5" wide, red mark #27. $275.00–295.00.

Plate 547. Figural matchbox holder, 3¼" tall, red mark #27. $150.00–175.00.

Plate 548. Figural tobacco jar, 4½" tall, red mark #27. $200.00–225.00.

Plate 549. Figural ashtray, 5" wide, red mark #27. $175.00–295.00.

Plate 550. Figural ashtray, 5" wide, red mark #27. $275.00–295.00.

Plates 551. Figural ashtray, 5" wide, red mark #27. $275.00–295.00.

Plate 553. Figural pipe holder and match holder, 3½" tall, red mark #27. $275.00–295.00.

Plate 552. Figural candy jar, 9½" tall, green mark #27. $275.00–295.00.

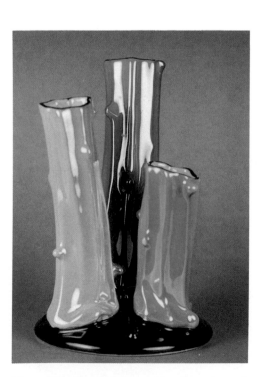

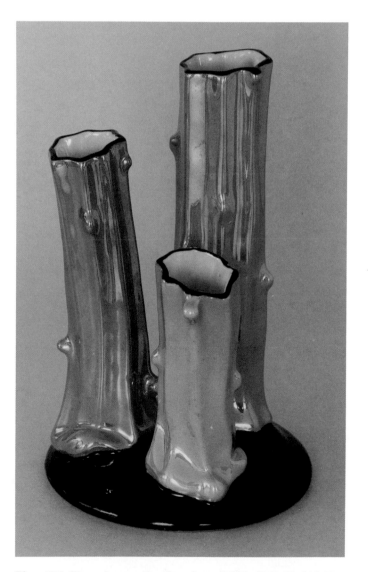

Plate 554. Figural vase, 6" tall, red mark #27. $175.00–195.00.

Plate 555. Figural vase, 6" tall, red mark #27. $175.00–195.00.

Plate 556. Figural vase, 10" tall, red mark
#27. $150.00–175.00.

Plate 557. Figural vase, 6¾" tall, red
mark #27. $125.00–135.00.

Plate 558. Figural vase, 5¼" tall, red
mark #27. $95.00–110.00.

Plate 559. Figural vase, 7" tall, green mark
#27. $200.00–225.00.

Plate 560. Figural vase, 5½" tall, red mark
#27. $150.00–175.00.

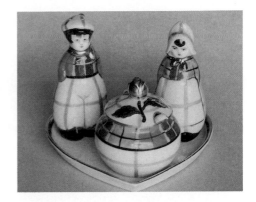

Plate 561. Figural condiment set: tray, 7" long, red mark #27. $175.00–195.00.

Plate 563. Figural condiment set: tray, 7" long, red mark #27. $175.00–195.00.

Plate 564. Figural condiment set: tray, 7½" long, green mark #27. $65.00–85.00.

Plate 565. Figural condiment set: tray, 7" long, green mark #27. $95.00–110.00.

Plate 567. Figural condiment set: tray, 7½" long, green mark #27. $95.00–110.00.

Plate 566. Figural condiment set, 4" tall, red mark #27. $195.00–225.00.

Plate 569. Figural condiment set, tray, 7½" long, green mark #27. $95.00–110.00.

Plate 568. Figural condiment set, red mark #27. $175.00–195.00.

Plate 570. Figural condiment set, red mark #27. $175.00–195.00.

Plate 571. Figural condiment set, green mark #27. $110.00–125.00.

Plate 572. Figural salt & pepper set, tray, 4¼" long, green mark #27. $95.00–110.00.

Plate 573. Figural salt & pepper set 2½" tall, green mark #27. $95.00–110.00.

Plates 574. Figural salt & pepper sets. Dutch girl, 3¾" tall, tray, 4¼" long, red mark #27. House, 2¼" tall, tray, 4¼" long, green mark #27. $95.00–110.00 each.

Plate 574A. Larkin catalog ad of item in plate #574.

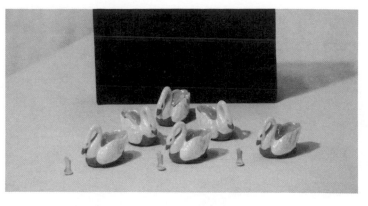

Plate 576. Figural open salt set with original box, master salt, 6"
long, green mark #27. $150.00–175.00.

Plate 575. Figural open salt set in original box master salt, 6"
long, individual salts, 2½" long, red mark #27. $150.00–175.00.

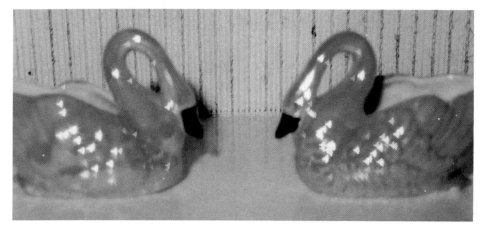

Plate 577. Figural open salts, 2½" long, green mark #27. $45.00–55.00 for pair.

Plate 578. Figural salt & pepper
set, red mark #27. $55.00–70.00.

Plate 580. Figural salt set, tray, 4¼" long,
red mark #27. $150.00–170.00.

Plate 579. Figural salt set, tray, 4¼" long, red mark #27. $150.00–170.00.

Plate 581. Figural open salt & pepper set, tray, 4¾" long, green mark #27 $75.00–95.00.

Plate 583. Figural wall pocket, 6½" wide, green mark #27. $250.00–275.00.

Plate 582. Figural salt set, tray, 4¼" long, red mark #27. $75.00–95.00.

Plate 585. Figural jam jar, 4½" tall, red mark #27. $50.00–65.00.

Plate 584. Figural wall pocket, 7½" long, red mark #27. $150.00–175.00.

Plate 586. Figural jam jars, left: 4¼" tall, red mark #27, $55.00–70.00.
Right: 5¼" tall, red mark #27, $45.00–60.00.

Plate 587. Figural jam jar, 5¼" tall, red mark #27. $60.00–75.00.

Plate 588. Figural jam jar, 5½" wide, red mark #27. $60.00–75.00.

Plate 589. Figural jam jar, 5½" tall, red mark #27. $45.00–60.00.

Plate 590. Figural sugar shaker, green mark #27. $100.00–140.00.

Plate 592. Figural cigarette holder, 4¼" tall, red mark #27. $115.00–125.00.

Plate 591. Figural spooner, 8¼" wide, green mark #27. $85.00–95.00.

Plate 593. Figural honey jar, 4½" tall, green mark #27. $65.00–80.00.

Plate 594. Figural honey jar, 4½" tall, red mark #27. $65.00–80.00.

Plate 595. Figural honey jar, 3½" tall, red mark #27. $70.00–85.00.

Plate 596. Figural honey jar, 3½" tall, red mark #27. $70.00–85.00.

Plate 597. Figural celery dish and individual salt, 12½" long, red mark #27. $95.00–115.00.

*Plate 598. Figural celery set, 13" long, red mark #27. $95.00–115.00.*

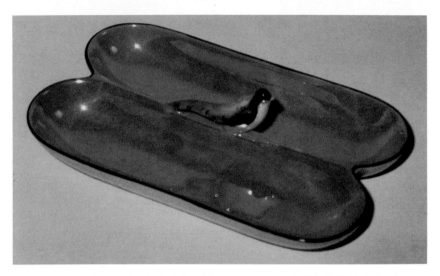

*Plate 599. Figural relish dish, 6" long, green mark #27. $95.00–115.00.*

*Plate 601. Figural relish dish, 6" long, green mark #27. $95.00–115.00.*

*Plate 600. Figural lemon dish, 5¾" wide, red mark #27.*
*$35.00–50.00.*

Plate 603. Figural lemon dish, 5¾" wide, red mark #27. $35.00–50.00.

Plate 602. Figural place card holder with original box, red mark #27. $160.00–175.00.

Plate 604. Figural place card holders, 1½" tall, red mark #27. $95.00–110.00.

Plate 605. Figural place card holders, 1½" tall, red mark #27. $110.00–125.00.

Plate 606. Figural cream & sugar set, sugar, 2" tall, red mark #27. $45.00–60.00.

Plate 607. Figural tea set, teapot, 6½" tall, green mark #27. $150.00–200.00.

Plate 608. Figural cream & sugar set, 4" tall, green mark #27. $45.00–60.00.

Plate 609. Figural tray, 8¼" long, red mark #27. $45.00–60.00.

Plate 610. Compote, relief molded, 5¾" tall, red mark #27. $100.00–125.00.

Plate 611. Vase, molded in relief, 7¾" tall, red mark #27. $145.00–160.00.

Plate 610A. Inside view of 610.

Plate 614. Vase, molded in relief, 7¾" tall, red mark #27. $145.00–160.00.

Plate 612. Vase, molded in relief, 5¼" tall, green mark #27. $145.00–160.00.

Plate 613. Vase, molded in relief, 7¾" tall, red mark #27. $145.00–160.00.

97

Plate 615. Wall pockets, molded in relief, 5½" long, green mark #27. $350.00–375.00 pair.

Plate 616. Wall pocket, molded in relief, red mark #27. $135.00–150.00.

Plate 617. Wall pocket, relief molded, 7½" long, green mark #27. $135.00–150.00.

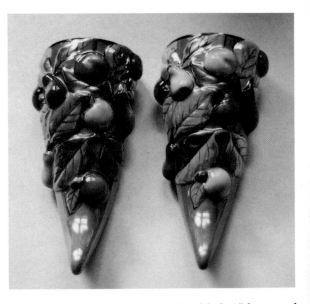

Plate 618. Wall pockets, relief molded, 8" long, red mark #27. $350.00–375.00 pair.

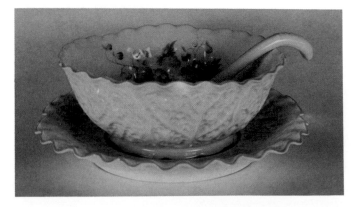

Plate 619. Sauce bowl, ladle and underplate, underplate, 6½" wide, red mark #50, molded in relief. $65.00–80.00.

Plate 620. Bowl, molded in relief, 6½" wide, green mark #27. $125.00–150.00.

Plate 621. Bowl, molded in relief, 7½" wide, green mark #27. $100.00–130.00.

Plate 622. Bowl, molded in relief, 7" wide, red mark #27. $125.00–150.00.

Plate 624. Bowl, molded in relief, 7" wide, red mark #27. $125.00–150.00.

Plate 623. Bowl, molded in relief, 6¾" wide, green mark #27. $95.00–110.00.

Plate 625. Bowl, molded in relief, 7¼" wide, red mark #27. $95.00–110.00.

Plate 626. Vase, moriage trim, 5" tall, green mark #27. $100.00–135.00.

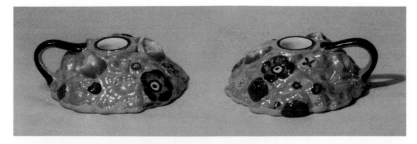

Plate 627. Pair of candlesticks, 4¾" wide, red mark #27. $210.00–230.00 pair.

Plate 628. Pair of candlesticks, 4¾" wide, green mark #27. $210.00–230.00 pair.

Plate 630. Bowl, silver overlay trim, 6¾" wide, red mark #27. $95.00–100.00.

Plate 629. Vase, 7¼" tall, same as plate #1417, souvenir of Windsor, Canada, red mark #27. $275.00–295.00.

Plate 631. Cosmetic jar, souvenir of Bermuda, 3" tall, same as plate # 495, red mark #27. $275.00–295.00.

Plate 632. Candy dish, gold etched, 6" long, mark #59. $75.00–100.00.

Plate 633. Salt & pepper set, 3¼" tall, souvenir of Niagara Falls, NY, green mark #27. $45.00–60.00.

Plate 634. Powder puff box, 3½" wide, souvenir of Standing Rock Wis. Dell, same as plate # 1225, red mark #27. $195.00–215.00.

Plate 635. Set of ashtrays, 4¼" wide, cigarette box wedgwood style, 4¼" long, green mark #27. $300.00–325.00 set.

Plate 636. Pair of wall plaques, wedgwood style, 5" long, green mark #27. $750.00–800.00 pair.

Plate 637. Lamp base, 11½" tall, wedgwood style, red mark #27. $475.00–500.00.

Plate 638. Vase, wedgwood style, 10" tall, green mark #27. $350.00–395.00.

Plate 639. Vase, wedgwood style, 12" tall, green mark #27. $450.00–495.00.

Plate 640. Vase, wedgwood style, 7" tall, red mark #50. $450.00–495.00.

Plate 641. Bowl, 9" wide, red mark #27. $75.00–95.00.

Plate 642. Bowl, 6½" wide, red mark #27. $45.00–60.00.

Plate 643. Bowl, 11" long, green mark #27. $75.00–95.00.

Plate 644. Bowl, 6½" wide, green mark #27. $45.00–60.00.

Plate 645. Bowl, 11½" wide, green mark #27. $75.00–95.00.

102

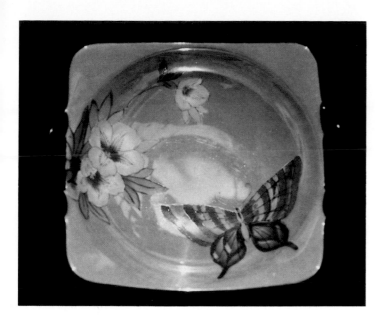

*Plate 646. Bowl, 6¾" wide, red mark #27. $50.00–60.00.*

*Plate 647. Bowl, 7½" wide, red mark #27. $45.00–60.00.*

*Plate 648. Bowl, 7½" wide, red mark #27. $45.00–60.00.*

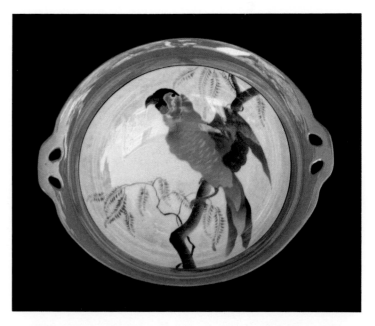

*Plate 649. Bowl, 8¾" wide, green mark #27. $60.00–75.00.*

Plate 650. Bowl, 9½" wide, red mark #27. $60.00–75.00.

Plate 651. Bowl, 8" wide, green mark #27. $60.00–75.00.

Plate 652. Lemon dish, 5½" wide, red mark #50. Bowl, 5¼" wide, red mark #27. $45.00–60.00 each.

Plate 653. Bowl, 4½" wide, red mark #27. $45.00–60.00.

Plate 654. Bowl, 7¼" wide, green mark #27. $45.00–60.00.

*Plate 655. Bowl, 7½" wide, green mark #27. $70.00–85.00.*

*Plate 656. Bowl, 7" wide, red mark #27. $45.00–60.00.*

*Plate 657. Bowl, 7¼" wide, red mark #27. $55.00–70.00.*

*Plate 658. Bowl, 8½" wide, red mark #27. $45.00–60.00.*

*Plate 659. Bowl, 9¼" wide, green mark #27. $75.00–90.00.*

*Plate 660. Bowl, 7" wide, green mark #27. $75.00–90.00.*

*Plate 661. Bowl, 10¼" wide, red mark #27. $75.00–90.00.*

Plate 662. Bowl, 9" wide, red mark #27. $55.00–70.00.

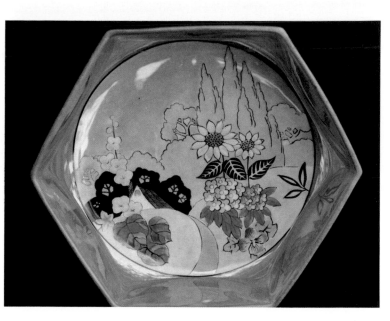

Plate 663. Bowl, 7½" wide, red mark #27. $75.00–90.00.

Plate 664. Bowl, 6¾" wide, red mark #27. $75.00–90.00.

Plate 665. Bowl, 10" wide, red mark #27. $75.00–90.00.

Plate 666. Bowl, 6¼" wide, green mark #27. $45.00–60.00.

Plate 667. Bowl, 6" wide, red mark #27. $45.00–60.00.

Plate 668. Bowl, 7¼" wide, green mark #27. $45.00–60.00.

Plate 669. Bowl, 7¼" wide, red mark #27. $45.00–60.00.

108

Plate 670. Bowl, 7¾" wide, red mark #27. $45.00–60.00.

Plate 671. Bowl, 7" wide, red mark #27. $75.00–90.00.

Plate 672. Bowl, 5½" wide, red mark #50. $75.00–90.00.

Plate 673. Bowl, 8¾" wide, green mark #27. $55.00–65.00.

Plate 674. Bowl, 8" wide, green mark #27. $55.00–65.00.

Plate 675. Bowl, 8¼" wide, red mark #52. $55.00–65.00.

Plate 676. Bowl, 7½" wide, red mark #27. $45.00–60.00.

Plate 677. Bowl, 8¼" wide, red mark #27. $55.00–65.00.

*Plate 678. Bowl, 6¾" wide, green mark #27. $75.00–90.00.*

*Plate 679. Bowl, 6½" wide, red mark #29. $75.00–90.00.*

*Plate 680. Bowl, 5½" wide, green mark #27. $75.00–90.00.*

*Plate 681. Bowl, 6¾" wide, red mark #27. $75.00–90.00.*

Plate 682. Bowl, 10" wide, green mark #27. Bowl, 12" wide, green mark #27. $60.00–70.00 each.

Plate 684. Bowl, 6½" wide, red mark #27. $45.00–60.00.

Plate 683. Bowl, 10" wide, red mark #27. $60.00–70.00.

Plate 685. Bowl, 10" wide, red mark #27. $60.00–70.00.

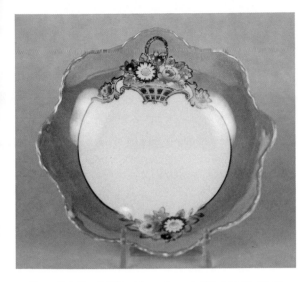

*Plate 686. Bowl, 5½" wide, red mark #27. $45.00–60.00.*

*Plate 687. Bowl, 8" wide, green mark #27. $45.00–60.00.*

*Plate 688. Bowl, 4¼" wide, red mark #27. $55.00–70.00.*

*Plate 689. Bowl, 7" wide, green mark #27. $45.00–70.00.*

*Plate 690. Bowl, 7½" wide, green mark #27. $75.00–90.00.*

Plate 691. Bowl, 8½" wide, red mark #27. $45.00–60.00.

Plate 692. Bowl, 4" wide, red mark #27. $55.00–70.00.

Plate 693. Bowl, 7½" wide, green mark #27. $60.00–75.00.

Plate 694. Bowl, 10½" long, green mark #27. $55.00–70.00.

Plate 695. Bowl, 8" wide, red mark #27. $40.00–50.00.

Plate 696. Bowl, 7" wide, red mark #27. $75.00–90.00.

Plate 697. Bowl, 7¼" wide, red mark #27. $75.00–90.00.

Plate 698. Bowl, 7½" wide, red mark #27. $75.00–90.00.

Plate 699. Bowl, 6" wide, red mark #27. $75.00–90.00.

*Plate 700. Bowl, 10½" wide, red mark #27. $75.00–90.00.*

*Plate 701. Bowl, 7½" wide, red mark #27. $75.00–90.00.*

*Plate 702. Bowl, 7" wide, red mark #27. $75.00–90.00.*

*Plate 703. Bowl, 8¼" wide, red mark #27. $75.00–90.00.*

*Plate 704. Bowl, 6¾" wide, red mark #27. $75.00–90.00.*

*Plate 705. Bowl, 4¼" wide, green mark #27. $45.00–60.00.*

*Plate 706. Bowl, 5½" wide, red mark #27. $75.00–90.00.*

*Plate 707. Bowl, 5½" wide, green mark #27. $45.00–60.00.*

*Plate 709. Bowl, 8¾" wide, green mark #27. $75.00–90.00.*

*Plate 708. Bowl, 10" wide, green mark #27. $60.00–75.00.*

*Plate 711. Bowl, 6¾" wide, green mark #27. $65.00–80.00.*

*Plate 710. Bowl, 9½" wide, red mark #27. $75.00–90.00.*

*Plate 712. Bowl, 8¼" wide, red mark #27. $65.00–80.00.*

*Plate 713. Bowl, 6¼" wide, red mark #27. $75.00–90.00.*

*Plate 714. Bowl, 7" wide, green mark #27. $45.00–60.00.*

*Plate 715. Bowl, 7½" wide, red mark #27. $55.00–70.00.*

Plate 717. Bowl, 7¾" wide, red mark #98. $45.00–60.00.

Plate 716. Bowl, 7½" wide, green mark #27. $75.00–90.00.

Plate 719. Bowl, 8½" wide, green mark #27. $45.00–60.00.

Plate 718. Bowl, 6¾" wide, red mark #27. $75.00–90.00.

Plate 720. Bowl, 6½" wide, red mark #27. $45.00–60.00.

Plate 721. Bowl, 7" wide, green mark #27. $75.00–90.00.

Plate 722. Bowl, 6" wide, red mark #27. $45.00–60.00.

Plate 723. Bowl, 4" wide, red mark #27. $65.00–80.00.

Plate 724. Bowl, 9¼" wide, green mark #27. $75.00–90.00.

Plate 725. Bowl, 5½" wide, red mark #27. $65.00–80.00.

Plate 726. Bowl, 6½" wide, red mark #27. $75.00–90.00.

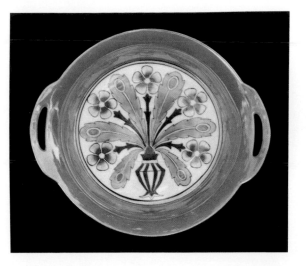

Plate 727. Bowl, 7¾" wide, red mark #27. $55.00–70.00.

Plate 728. Bowl, 5¾" wide, red mark #27. Bowl, 6" wide, red mark #27. $45.00–60.00 each.

Plate 729. Bowl, 5½" wide, red mark #27. $55.00–70.00.

Plate 730. Bowl, 7¼" wide, red mark #27. $55.00–70.00.

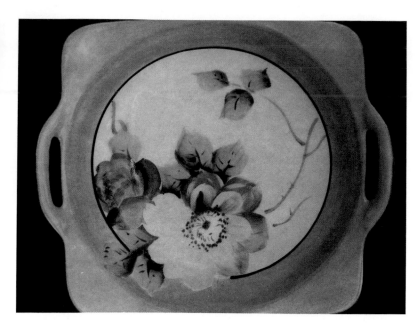

Plate 731. Bowl, 6½" wide, green mark #27. $60.00–75.00.

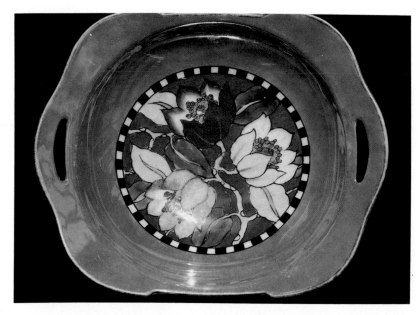

Plate 734. Bowl, 9" wide, red mark #27. $55.00–70.00.

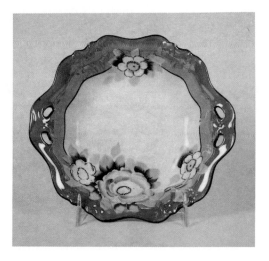

Plate 732. Bowl, 6¼" wide, green mark #27. $55.00–70.00.

Plate 733. Bowl, 6" wide, red mark #27. $45.00–60.00.

Plate 735. Bowl, 6¾" wide, red mark #27. $55.00–70.00.

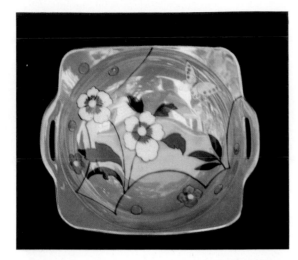

Plate 736. Bowl, 6½" wide, red mark #27. $45.00–60.00.

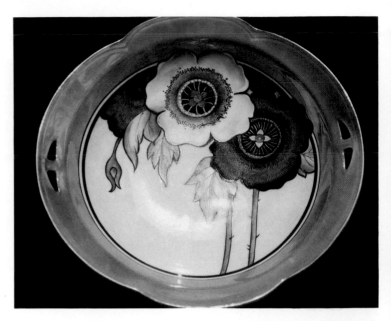

Plate 737. Bowl, 8¼" wide, red mark #27. $75.00–90.00.

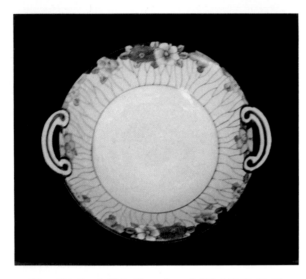

Plate 738. Bowl, 6¾" wide, red mark #27. $45.00–60.00.

Plate 739. Bowl, 8¾" wide, green mark #27. $55.00–70.00.

Plate 740. Bowl, 7¼" wide, green mark #27. $55.00–70.00.

Plate 741. Bowl, 7" wide, green mark #27. $45.00–60.00.

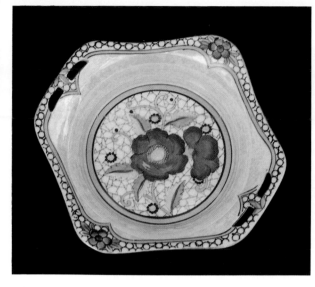

Plate 742. Bowl, 7½" wide, green mark #27. $45.00–60.00.

Plate 743. Bowl, 8" wide, red mark #27. $55.00–70.00.

Plate 744. Bowl, 7" wide, red mark #27. $55.00–70.00.

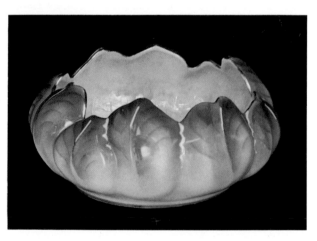

Plate 745. Bowl, 7¼" wide, red mark #27. $55.00–70.00.

Plate 746. Bowl, 8¼" wide, green mark #27. $50.00–65.00.

Plate 747. Bowl, 8½" wide, green mark #27. $55.00–70.00.

Plate 748. Bowl, 6½" wide, red mark #27. $45.00–60.00.

Plate 749. Bowl, 6½" wide, red mark #27. $60.00–75.00.

Plate 750. Bowl, 5" wide, green mark #27. Bowl, 6" wide, green mark #27. $45.00–60.00 each.

Plate 751. Bowl, 7½" wide, green mark #27. $60.00–75.00.

Plate 752. Bowl, 8" wide, red mark #27. $60.00–75.00.

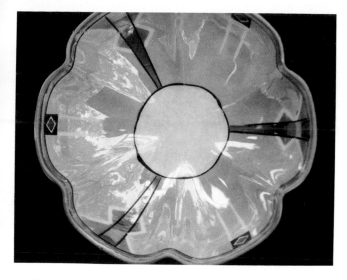

*Plate 753. Bowl, 5½" wide, red mark #27. $70.00–85.00.*

*Plate 754. Bowl, 7" wide, red mark #27. $45.00–60.00.*

*Plate 755. Bowl, 5½" wide, red mark #27.*
*$75.00–90.00.*

*Plate 756. Bowl, 8¾" wide, green mark #27. $55.00–70.00.*

*Plate 757. Bowl, 6½" wide, green mark #27. $45.00–60.00.*

*Plate 758. Bowl, 9½" wide, green mark #27. $55.00–70.00.*

Plate 759. Bowl, 8" wide, red mark #27. $75.00–90.00.

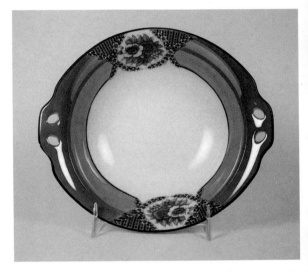

Plate 760. Covered bowl, 5¼" tall, green mark #27. $55.00–70.00.

Plate 761. Bowl, 9¾" wide, green mark #27. $55.00–70.00.

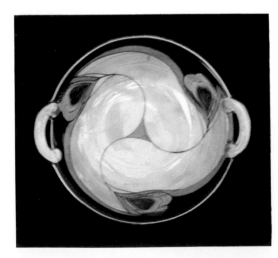

Plate 762. Bowl, 7" wide, red mark #27. $45.00–60.00.

Plate 763. Bowl, 6¾" wide, green mark #27. $55.00–70.00.

Plate 764. Bowl with underplate, bowl, 7½" wide, green mark #27. $40.00–60.00.

Plate 765. Bowl, 7½" wide, green mark #27. $45.00–60.00.

Plate 766. Bowl, 7" wide, green mark #27. $55.00–70.00.

Plate 767. Bowl, 7½" wide, green mark #27. $55.00–70.00.

Plate 768. Candy dish, 4½" long, green mark #27. $20.00–30.00.

Plate 769. Bowl, 9½" wide, green mark #27. $50.00–65.00.

Plate 770. Bowl, 9" wide, green mark #27. $75.00–90.00.

Plate 771. Candy dish, 9½" wide, red mark #27. $45.00–60.00.

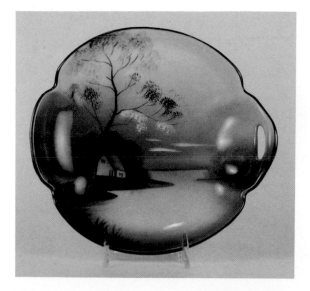

Plate 772. Candy dish, 5½" wide, red mark #27. $45.00–60.00.

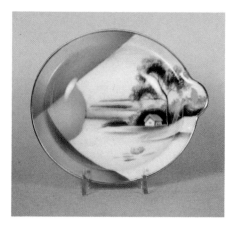

Plate 773. Candy dish, 5¾" wide, red mark #27. $45.00–60.00.

Plate 774. Candy dish, 6½" long, red mark #27. $45.00–60.00.

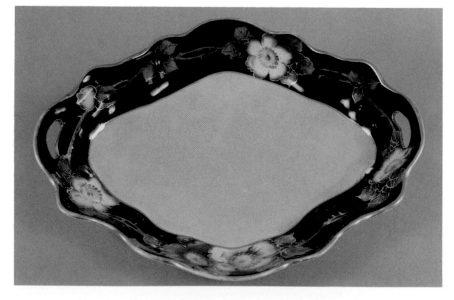

Plate 775. Bowl, 10½" wide, green mark #27. $45.00–60.00.

Plate 776. Candy dish, 7" wide, red mark #27. $45.00–60.00.

Plate 777. Bowl, 7¼" wide, red mark #27. $45.00–60.00.

Plate 778. Candy dish, 10" wide, green mark #27. $50.00–65.00.

Plate 779. Left: candy dish, 5" wide, green mark #27. $150.00–180.00. Right: candy dish, 7½" wide, green mark #27. $45.00–60.00.

Plate 780. Candy dish, 8½" long, red mark #27. $75.00–95.00.

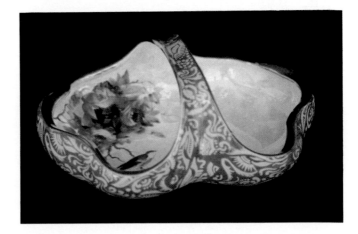

Plate 781. Candy dish, 7½" long, red mark #27. $95.00–110.00.

*Plate 782. Candy dish, 6" wide, green mark #27. $45.00–60.00.*

*Plate 783. Bowl, 9¾" wide, red mark #27. $55.00–70.00.*

*Plate 784. Bowl, 6¼" wide, red mark #27. $45.00–60.00.*

*Plate 785. Candy dish, 7" long, red mark #27. $15.00–20.00.*

*Plate 786. Candy dish, 9" wide, red mark #27. $45.00–60.00.*

*Plate 787. Candy dish, 9¼" wide, red mark #27. $45.00–60.00.*

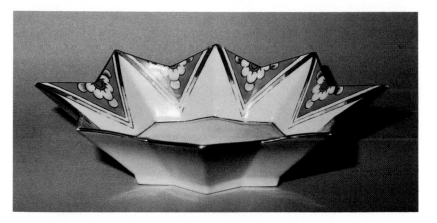

Plate 788. Candy dish, 9¾" wide, red mark #27. $85.00–105.00.

Plate 789. Candy dish, 6½" wide, red mark #27. $85.00–105.00.

Plate 790. Candy dish, 7¼" wide, red mark #27. $85.00–105.00.

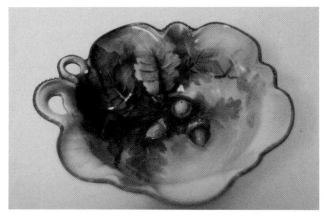

Plate 791. Candy dish, 6½" wide, green mark #27. $45.00–60.00.

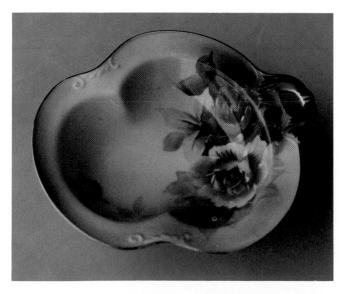

Plate 792. Candy dish, 6½" wide, red mark #27. $45.00–60.00.

Plate 793. Candy dish, 8½" wide, red mark #27. $95.00–115.00.

Plate 794. Candy dish, 5¾" wide, red mark #27. $45.00–60.00.

Plate 795. Candy dish, 5¾" wide, red mark #50. $75.00–90.00.

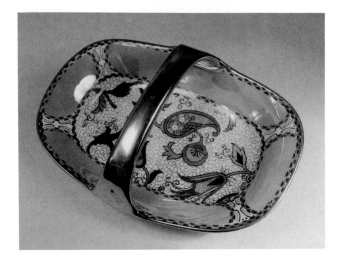

Plate 796. Candy dish, 7¾" long, green mark #27. $55.00–70.00.

Plate 797. Candy dish, 6" wide, green mark #27. $45.00–60.00.

Plate 798. Candy dish, 8¾" long, red mark #27. $100.00–125.00.

Plate 799. Candy dish, 5½" diameter, green mark #27. $35.00–45.00.

Plate 800. Candy dish, 5" long, red mark #27. $65.00–75.00.

Plate 801. Candy dish, 7" wide, green mark #27. $55.00–65.00.

Plate 802. Candy dish, 4½" tall, red mark #27. $55.00–65.00.

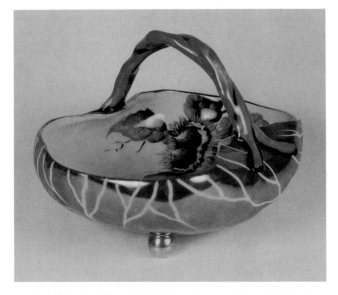

Plate 803. Candy dish, 7½" wide, red mark #27. $55.00–65.00.

Plate 804. Candy dish, 6½" long, red mark #27. $65.00–80.00.

Plate 805. Candy dish, 5½" long, red mark #27. $55.00–65.00.

Plate 806. Candy dish, 8" long, red mark #27. $55.00–65.00.

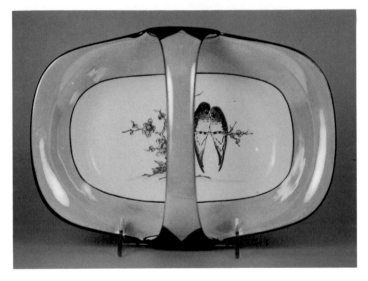

Plate 807. Candy dish, 9¾" long, green mark #38. $55.00–65.00.

Plate 808. Candy dish, 5½" tall, red mark #27. $55.00–65.00.

Plate 809. Candy dish, 3" tall, red mark #27. $55.00–65.00.

Plate 810. Candy dish, 6¼" long, red mark #27. $55.00–65.00.

*Plate 811. Candy dish, 6¼" long, red mark #27. $75.00–85.00.*

*Plate 812. Candy dish, 7" wide, red mark #27. $65.00–80.00.*

*Plate 814. Candy dish, 8½" long, red mark #27. $50.00–65.00.*

*Plate 813. Candy dish, 6¼" wide, red mark #27. $45.00–60.00.*

*Plate 815. Candy dish, 6" long, green mark #27. $55.00–65.00.*

*Plate 816. Covered candy jar, 9" tall, green mark #27. $175.00–200.00.*

137

Plate 817. Candy dish, 8" long, red mark #27. $55.00–65.00.

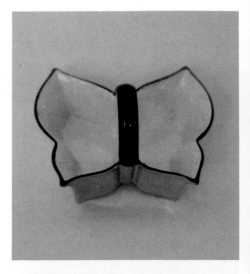

Plate 818. Candy dish, 5½" wide, red mark #27. $40.00–55.00.

Plate 819. Candy dish, 9" long, red mark #27. $65.00–75.00.

Plate 820. Candy dish, 4¾" tall, red mark #27. $55.00–65.00.

Plate 821. Candy dish, 9" long, red mark #27. $65.00–75.00.

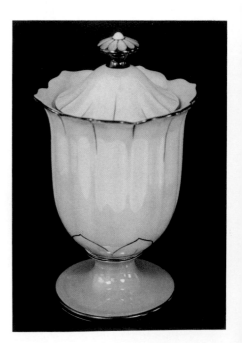

Plate 822. Covered candy jar, 8" tall, green mark #27. $110.00–135.00.

*Plate 823. Candy jar, 9" tall, green mark #27. $200.00–250.00.*

*Plate 824. Candy jar, 5½" tall, red mark #27. $135.00–160.00.*

*Plate 825. Candy jar, 6" tall, red mark #27. $65.00–75.00.*

*Plate 826. (Left to right) Candy dish, 8" wide, green mark #27. $45.00–60.00. Lemon dish, 6" wide, red mark #27. $30.00–40.00. Candy dish, 6¾" wide, red mark #27. $30.00–40.00.*

139

Plate 827. Covered candy dish, 6¾" wide, red mark #27. $125.00–150.00.

Plate 828. Covered candy dish, 5¼" wide, red mark #27. $125.00–150.00.

Plate 829. Covered candy dish, 5¼" wide, red mark #27. $125.00–150.00.

Plate 830. Covered candy dish, 6¼" wide, red mark #27. $125.00–150.00.

Plate 831. Covered candy dish, 6¼" wide, red mark #27. $125.00–150.00.

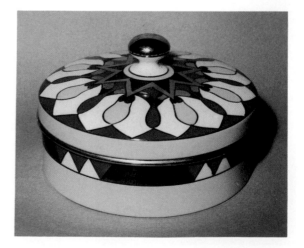

Plate 832. Covered candy dish, 6¼" wide, red mark #27. $125.00–150.00.

Plate 834. Nappy, 6" wide, red mark #27. $45.00–60.00.

Plate 833. Covered candy dish, 6" wide, green mark #27. $100.00–115.00.

Plate 836. Covered candy dish, 6½" wide, red mark #27. $100.00–115.00.

Plate 835. Covered candy dish, 8" wide, red mark #27. $100.00–115.00.

Plate 837. Covered candy dish, 7½" wide, red mark #50. $100.00–115.00.

Plate 838. Nappy, 6" wide, red mark #27. $55.00–70.00.

Plate 839. Cream & sugar set, sugar bowl, 5" tall, red mark #27. Jam jar, 5½" tall, red mark #27. $75.00–95.00.

Plate 840. Cream & sugar set, sugar bowl, 4½" tall, red mark #27. $45.00–60.00.

Plate 841. Condiment set, tray, 5" wide, green mark #27. $65.00–80.00.

Plate 842. Condiment set, tray, 4¾" wide, red mark #27. $65.00–80.00.

Plate 843. Cream & sugar set, sugar bowl, 2¼" tall, green mark #27. $35.00–45.00.

Plate 844. Cream & sugar set, sugar bowl, 5" tall, red mark #27. $40.00–60.00.

Plate 845. Condiment set, tray, 3" wide, green mark #27. $45.00–60.00.

Plate 846. Condiment set, 3¼" tall, red mark #27. $125.00–140.00.

Plate 847. Cream & sugar set, sugar bowl, 4½" tall, red mark #29. $40.00–60.00.

Plate 848. Cream & sugar set, sugar bowl, 6" wide, red mark #27. $45.00–60.00.

Plate 849. Condiment set, green mark #27. $35.00–45.00.

*Plate 850. Cream & sugar set, 4½" tall, green mark #27. $60.00–80.00.*

*Plate 851. Cream & sugar set, sugar bowl, 6" wide, green mark #27. $55.00–70.00.*

*Plate 852. Creamer, red mark #27. $30.00–40.00.*

*Plate 853. Berry sugar & cream set, 6½" tall, red mark #27. $60.00–70.00.*

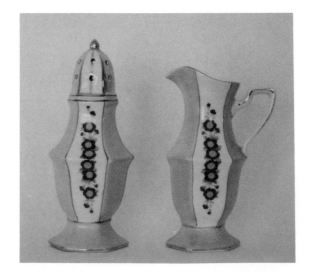

*Plate 854. Berry sugar & cream set, sugar shaker, 6½" tall, red mark #27. $60.00–70.00.*

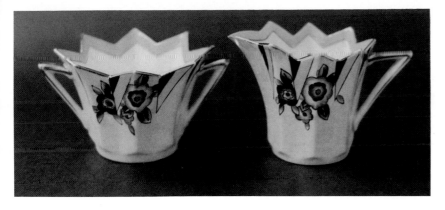

Plate 855. Cream & sugar set, creamer, 3¼" tall, red mark #27. $60.00–70.00.

Plate 856. Cream & sugar set, creamer, 2½" tall, green mark #27. $45.00–60.00.

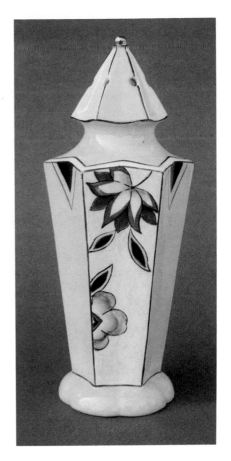

Plate 857. Sugar shaker, 6¾" tall, red mark #27. $35.00–40.00.

Plate 858. Berry sugar & creamer set, 6½" tall, red mark #27. Berry sugar & creamer set, 7" tall, red mark #27. $60.00–70.00 each set.

Plate 859. Cream & sugar set, sugar bowl, 4½" tall, green mark #38. Mustard jar, 3" tall, green mark #38. $60.00–70.00.

Plate 860. Cream & sugar set, sugar bowl, 3¼" tall, green mark #21. $50.00–70.00.

Plate 861. Berry sugar & cream set, sugar shaker, 6½" tall, red mark #27. $70.00–90.00.

Plate 862. Berry sugar & cream set, sugar shaker, 6½" tall, red mark #27. $90.00–110.00.

Plate 863. Berry sugar & cream set, sugar shaker, 6½" tall, red mark #27. $125.00–135.00.

Plate 864. Cream & sugar set, 3½" tall, red mark #27. $75.00–90.00.

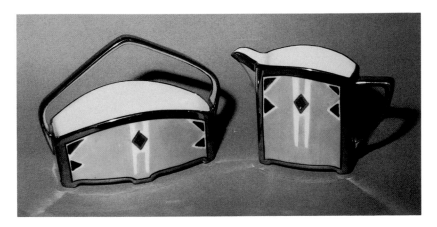

Plate 865. Cream & sugar set, 3½" tall, red mark #27. $75.00–90.00.

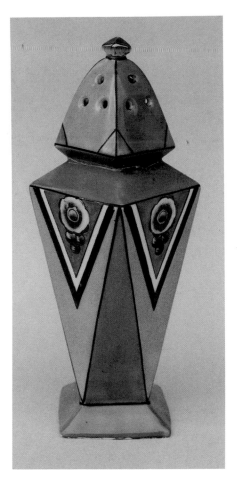

Plate 866. Sugar shaker, 7" tall, red mark #27. $40.00–45.00.

Plate 867. Berry sugar & cream set, sugar shaker, 6½" tall, red mark #27. $90.00–125.00.

Plate 868. Berry sugar & cream set, sugar shaker, 6½" tall, red mark #27. $70.00–90.00.

Plate 369. Cream & sugar set, sugar bowl, 4½" wide, red mark #52. $45.00–60.00.

Plate 870. Condiment set, 5½" wide, red mark #27. $75.00–95.00.

Plate 871. Jam jar, underplate 6½" wide, red mark #27. Condiment set, 4½" wide, red mark #27. Left, $45.00–60.00; right, $75.00–95.00.

Plate 872. Condiment set, 5½" wide, red mark #27. $75.00–95.00.

Plate 873. Berry sugar & cream set, sugar shaker, 6½" tall, red mark #27. $60.00–70.00.

Plate 874. Berry sugar & cream set, sugar shaker, 6½" tall, red mark #27. $60.00–70.00.

148

Plate 875. Creamer, 3½" tall, green mark #27. $60.00–70.00.

Plate 876. Berry sugar & creamer set, sugar shaker, 7" tall, red mark #27. $75.00–90.00.

Plate 877. Condiment set, tray, 7½" long, green mark #27. $175.00–195.00.

Plate 878. Sauce dish, 5¼" wide, green mark #27. $30.00–40.00.

Plate 879. Condiment set, tray, 5" wide, green mark #27. Open sugar, 6" wide, green mark #27. Left, $65.00–85.00; right, $20.00–25.00.

Plate 880. Salt & pepper set, 2" tall, green mark #27. $30.00–40.00.

Plate 881. *Individual salts, 2½" long, in original box, red mark #27. $95.00–105.00.*

Plate 882. *Condiment set, tray, 4¼" wide, red mark #27. $75.00–95.00.*

Plate 884. *Sauce dish, 5½" wide, red mark #27. $25.00–35.00.*

Plate 883. *Cream & sugar set, sugar bowl, 3" tall, red mark #27. $45.00–60.00.*

Plate 885. *Salt & pepper set, 3" wide, red mark #27. Condiment set, 7½" long, green mark #38. Condiment set, 4" wide, green mark #27. Left, $30.00–40.00; center, $70.00–90.00; right, $70.00–95.00.*

Plate 886. Cream & sugar set, sugar, 2½" tall, red mark #50. $60.00–70.00.

Plate 887. Sauce dish, 3¾" tall, red mark #27. $50.00–65.00.

Plate 888. Sauce dish, underplate, 6¼" wide, red mark #27. $55.00–70.00.

Plate 889. Bowl, 5¾" wide, green mark #27. Condiment set, 7½" long, green mark #27. Left, $20.00–30.00; right, $75.00–95.00.

Plate 890. Salt & pepper set, tray, 5¼" long, green mark #27. $60.00–70.00.

Plate 891. Sauce dish, underplate, 6½" wide, red mark #27. $60.00–70.00.

Plate 892. Sauce dish, underplate, 6¼" wide, red mark #27. $60.00–75.00.

Plate 893. Cream & sugar set, creamer, 2½" tall, red mark #27. $50.00–70.00.

Plate 895. Mayonnaise set, underplate, 6¾" wide, green mark #27. $50.00–65.00.

Plate 894. Condiment set, tray, 7½" long, red mark #27. $75.00–95.00.

Plate 896. Condiment set, tray, 7½" long, red mark #27. $75.00–95.00.

Plate 897. Sauce dish, 3½" tall, green mark #27. $45.00–50.00.

Plate 898. Condiment set, tray, 7½" long, green mark #27. $75.00–95.00.

152

*Plate 899. Sauce dish, 3¼" tall, red mark #27. $55.00–70.00.*

*Plate 900. Open salt & pepper set, tray, 4¼" long, green mark #27. $55.00–70.00.*

*Plate 901. Sauce dish, underplate, 6¼" wide, red mark #27. $55.00–70.00.*

*Plate 902. Mayonnaise set, underplate, 6" wide, green mark #27. $50.00–65.00.*

*Plate 903. Mayonnaise set, underplate, 6½" wide, red mark #27. $50.00–60.00.*

*Plate 904. Mayonnaise set, 5" wide, red mark #27. $50.00–60.00.*

Plate 905. Sauce dish, under plate, 6" wide, red mark #27. $55.00–70.00.

Plate 906. Sauce dish, 5" wide, green mark #27. $50.00–60.00.

Plate 907. Mayonnaise set, underplate, 6" wide, green mark #27. $55.00–70.00.

Plate 908. Trivet, 6" wide, red mark #27. $130.00–160.00.

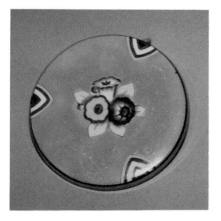

Plate 909. Trivet, 5¾" wide, red mark #27. $55.00–70.00.

Plate 910. Sauce dish, underplate, 7¼" wide, green mark #27. $50.00–60.00.

Plate 911. Sauce dish, 3¼" tall, green mark #27. $55.00–70.00.

Plate 912. Mayonnaise set, underplate, 5½" wide, red mark #27. $55.00–70.00.

Plate 914. Trivet, 5" wide, green mark #27. $55.00–75.00.

Plate 913. Mayonnaise set, underplate, 4½" wide, green mark #27. $55.00–70.00.

Plate 915. Trivet, 5¾" wide, green mark #27. $45.00–60.00.

Plate 916. Trivet, 6" wide, green mark #27. $125.00–140.00.

Plate 917. Trivet, 6½" wide, green mark #27. $115.00–125.00.

Plate 918. Covered butter dish, 6½" wide, red mark #27. $60.00–85.00.

Plate 919. Covered butter dish, 6½" wide, red mark #27. $60.00–85.00.

Plate 920. Covered butter dish, 6½" wide, red mark #27. $60.00–85.00.

Plate 921. Butter tub, 5¼" wide, red mark #27. Sugar bowl, 4" tall, red mark #27. $45.00–65.00.

Plate 922. Egg warmer, 6" wide, green mark #27. $85.00–95.00.

Plate 923. Covered butter dish, 6" wide, Azalea pattern, red mark #27. $60.00–85.00.

Plate 924. Covered butter dish, 6½" wide, red mark #27. $60.00–85.00.

Plate 925. Covered butter dish, 7½" wide, red mark #27. $60.00–85.00.

Plate 926. Slanted cheese, 8" long, red mark #27. $75.00–90.00.

Plate 927. Mustard jar, 3½" tall, red mark #27. $10.00–15.00.

Plate 928. Mint basket set, large basket, 5½" tall, small baskets, 2½" tall, green mark #27. $125.00–135.00 set.

157

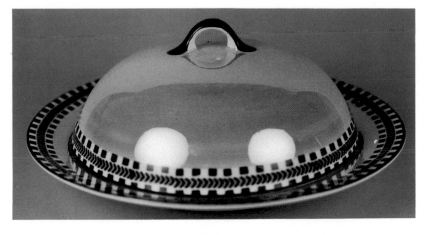

Plate 929. Pancake server, 7¾" wide, green mark #27. $55.00–65.00.

Plate 930. Jam jar, 5½" tall, red mark #27. $50.00–65.00.

Plate 931. Jam jar, 5½" tall, green mark #27. $65.00–75.00.

Plate 932. Syrup, 4½" tall, green mark #27. $55.00–70.00.

Plate 933. Sweetmeat set, 9¾" wide, red mark #27. $85.00–95.00.

Plate 934. Jam jar, 5½" tall, green mark #27. $60.00–70.00.

*Plate 935. Coaster, 4½" wide, red mark #27. $10.00–15.00.*

*Plate 936. Ice cream set, tray, 12½" long, green mark #27. $125.00–135.00.*

*Plate 937. Jam jar, 4¾" tall, green mark #27. $60.00–70.00.*

*Plate 938. Napkin rings, 2½" wide, red mark #27. $70.00–80.00 pair.*

*Plate 940. Jam jar, 4¾" tall, green mark #27. $60.00–70.00.*

*Plate 939. Ice cream set, tray, 12½" long, green mark #27. $125.00–135.00.*

Plate 941. Syrup, 4" tall, red mark #27. $50.00–60.00.

Plate 942. Syrup, 3¾" tall, green mark #27. $50.00–60.00.

Plate 943. Lemon dish, 6¼" wide, red mark #27. $45.00–60.00.

Plate 944. Lemon dish, 5½" wide, red mark #27. $45.00–60.00.

Plate 945. Lemon dish, 5½" wide, green mark #27. $125.00–135.00.

Plate 946. Ice cream set, large tray, 12½" long, green mark #27. $100.00–115.00.

Plate 947. Salad bowl, 8" wide, red mark #27. $100.00–125.00.

Plate 948. Lemon dish, 5½" wide, red mark #27. $40.00–60.00.

Plate 947A. Top view of 947.

Plate 949. Salad set, bowl, 12" long, red mark #27. $125.00–160.00.

Plate 950. Lemon dish, 6" wide, red mark #27. $45.00–60.00.

Plate 949A. Another view of 949.

Plate 951. Salad bowl, 10" wide, red mark #27. $125.00–160.00.

Plate 952. Salad bowl, 9" wide, green mark #27. $60.00–75.00.

Plate 953. Lemon dish, 4¼" wide, red mark #27. $45.00–60.00.

Plate 954. Salad bowl, 9½" long, red mark #29. $85.00–100.00.

Plate 955. Salad set, large bowl, 10" wide, red mark #27. $70.00–85.00.

Plate 956. Lemon dish, 5½" wide, red mark #27. $45.00–60.00.

162

Plate 958. Lemon dish, 6" wide, red mark #27. $45.00–60.00.

Plate 957. Salad set, large bowl, 9½" wide, green mark #27. $70.00–85.00.

Plate 960. Lemon dish, 5¾" wide, red mark #27. $45.00–60.00.

Plate 959. Lemon dish, 5½" wide, red mark #27. $45.00–60.00. Similar to plate 963, finial is different.

Plate 962. Lemon dish, 4½" wide, red mark #27. $45.00–60.00.

Plate 961. Candy dish, 6" long, red mark #27. Lemon dish, 5½" wide, red mark #27. Left, $30.00–40.00; right, $45.00–60.00.

Plate 963. Lemon dish, 6¼" wide, red mark #27. $45.00–60.00.

Plate 964. Lemon dish, 5½" wide, red mark #27. $45.00–60.00.

Plate 966. Lemon dish, 5¼" wide, red mark #27. $45.00–60.00.

Plate 965. Mustard jar, 3" tall, red mark #27. Lemon dish, 5½" wide, red mark #27. Left, $15.00–25.00; right, $40.00–55.00.

Plate 967. Lemon dish, 5½" wide, red mark #27. $45.00–60.00.

Plate 968. Lemon dish, 5½" wide, red mark #27. $45.00–60.00.

Plate 969. Lemon dish, 6½" wide, green mark #27. $125.00–140.00.

Plate 970. Pitcher, 7" tall, red mark #27. $60.00–75.00.

Plate 971. Lemon dish, 6¼" wide, green mark #27. $45.00–60.00.

Plate 972. Covered pitcher, 4½" tall, green mark #27. $20.00–30.00.

Plate 973. Candy dish, 6½" long, red mark #29. Lemon dish, 5¾" wide, red mark #29. Left, 20.00–30.00; right, 45.00–60.00.

Plate 974. Pitcher, 7½" tall, red mark #27. $160.00–200.00.

*Plate 975. Lemon dish, 5½" wide, red mark #27. $45.00–60.00.*

*Plate 976. Pitcher, 5½" tall, green mark #27. $25.00–40.00.*

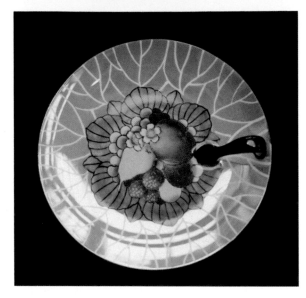

*Plate 977. Lemon dish, 6¼" wide, red mark #27. $45.00–60.00.*

*Plate 978. Lemon dish, 5½" wide, red mark #27. $45.00–60.00.*

*Plate 979. Luncheon set, consists of six plates, six cups & saucers, plates are 7¼" wide, green mark #27. $150.00–175.00.*

*Plate 980. Lemon dish, 6½" wide, red mark #27. $45.00–60.00.*

*Plate 981. Lemon dish, 6½" wide, red mark #27. $45.00–60.00.*

*Plate 982. Slanted cheese, 8" long, red mark #27. $75.00–85.00.*

*Plate 983. Lemon dish, 6" wide, green mark #27. $45.00–60.00.*

*Plate 984. Potpourri jar, 4¼" tall, green mark #27. $75.00–85.00.*

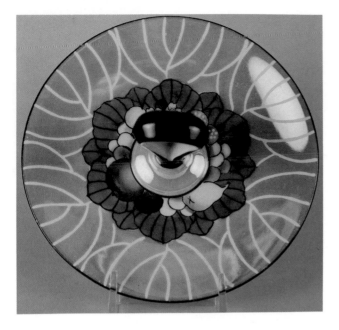

Plate 985. *Lemon dish, 5¼" wide, red mark #27. $45.00–60.00.*

Plate 986. *Potpourri jar, 5½" tall, red mark #27. (inner cover shown on right). $70.00–80.00.*

Plate 987. *Potpourri jar, 7¾" tall, red mark #27. Potpourri jar, 6¾" tall, red mark #27. $100.00–140.00 each.*

Plate 988. *Potpourri jar, 7¼" tall, red mark #27. $100.00–140.00.*

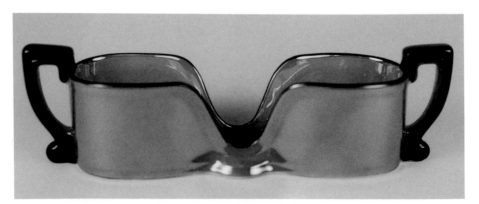

Plate 989. *Spooner, 8" long, green mark #27. $40.00–50.00.*

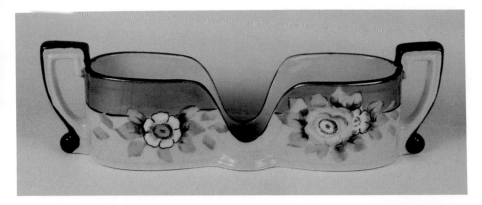

Plate 990. Spooner, 8" long, green mark #38. $40.00–50.00.

Plate 991. Spooner, 4¾" long, green mark #27. $40.00–50.00.

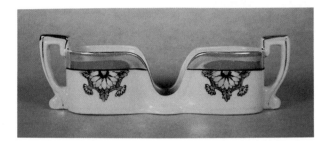

Plate 992. Spooner, 8" long, green mark #27. $40.00–50.00.

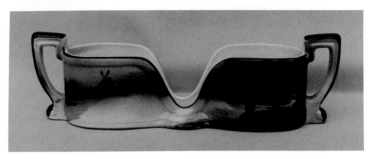

Plate 993. Spooner, 8" long, red mark #27. $40.00–50.00.

Plate 994. Spooner, 8" long, red mark #27. $40.00–50.00.

Plate 995. Candlestick, 8¼" tall, green mark #27. $70.00–75.00.

Plate 996. Cake plate, 7¼" wide, red mark #52. $10.00–15.00 each.

169

Plate 997. Pair of candlesticks, 5½" tall, red mark #27. $245.00–275.00 pair.

Plate 998. Candlestick, 5¼" tall, red mark #27. $55.00–70.00.

Plate 999. Pair of chambersticks, 2" tall, red mark #27. $60.00–80.00 pair.

Plate 1000. Chamberstick, 2" tall, green mark #27. $195.00–210.00.

Plate 1001. Pair of candlesticks, 7½" tall, green mark #27. $150.00–170.00 pair.

Plate 1002. Pair of candlesticks, 5½" tall, red mark #27. $150.00–170.00 pair.

Plate 1003. Pair of candlesticks, 7½" tall, green mark #27. $150.00–170.00 pair.

Plate 1004. Pair of candlesticks, 5¼" tall, green mark #27. $100.00–120.00 pair.

Plate 1005. Pair of chambersticks, 6" tall, green mark #27. $150.00–170.00 pair.

Plate 1006. Chamberstick, 4¾" tall, green mark #27. $75.00–85.00.

Plate 1007. Pair of candlesticks, 4¼" tall, red mark #27. $110.00–125.00 pair.

Plate 1008. Chamberstick, 2¾" tall, green mark #27. $60.00–80.00.

171

Plate 1009. Punch bowl set, 12¼" tall, set comes with 10 cups, green mark #27. $850.00–950.00.

Plate 1010. Cookie or biscuit jar, 8" tall, green mark #27. $135.00–160.00.

Plate 1011. Cracker jar, red mark #27. $75.00–95.00.

Plate 1012. Cookie or biscuit jar, 7" tall, green mark #27. $175.00–200.00.

Plate 1013. Pedestalled punch bowl & matching candlesticks, 3½" tall, bowl, 9½" diameter, excluding handles, red mark #27. $550.00–600.00 set.

172

Plate 1014. Cookie jar, 7" tall, green mark #27. Matching cup & saucer, green mark #27. Relish dish, 8" long, green mark #27. $100.00–115.00.

Plate 1015. Flower pot, 4½" tall, red mark #27. $150.00–180.00.

Plate 1016. Hanging planter, 5" tall, red mark #27. $150.00–180.00.

Plate 1017. Ferner, 8¼" long, red mark #27. $85.00–100.00.

Plate 1018. Hanging planter, 5" tall, red mark #27. $150.00–180.00.

Plate 1019. Ferner, 6½" wide, green mark #27. $85.00–100.00.

173

*Plate 1020. Sandwich plate, 9¼" wide, red mark #27. $60.00–75.00.*

*Plate 1021. Sandwich plate, 8¾" wide, red mark #27. $60.00–75.00.*

*Plate 1022. Sandwich plate, 9½" wide, red mark #27. $40.00–50.00.*

*Plate 1023. Sandwich plate, 10¼" wide, gold mark #59. $55.00–70.00.*

*Plate 1024. Sandwich plate, 7¾" wide, red mark #27. $60.00–75.00.*

Plate 1025. Sandwich plate, 7¾" wide, red mark #34. $40.00–50.00.

Plate 1026. Sandwich plate, 7¾" wide, red mark #27. $45.00–55.00.

Plate 1027. Celery dish, 12" long, red mark #27. $25.00–40.00.

Plate 1028. Sandwich plate, 7¾" wide, red mark #29. $45.00–55.00.

Plate 1029. Serving dish, 7¾" wide, red mark #27. $60.00–75.00.

*Plate 1030. Sandwich plate, 8" wide, red mark #27. $110.00–130.00.*

*Plate 1031. Serving dish, 7¾" wide, red mark #29. $40.00–50.00.*

*Plate 1032. Celery dish, 13½" long, red mark #27. $25.00–40.00.*

*Plate 1033. Sandwich plate, 8" wide, red mark #27. $45.00–55.00.*

*Plate 1034. Serving dish, 7¾" wide, red mark #27. $60.00–75.00.*

*Plate 1035. Serving dish, 7¼" wide, green mark #27. $45.00–60.00.*

*Plate 1036. Serving dish, 7½" wide, green mark #27. $45.00–60.00.*

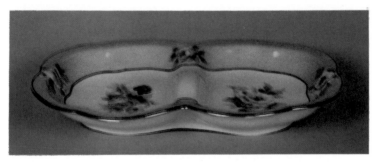

*Plate 1037. Relish dish, 8½" long, red mark #27. $45.00–55.00.*

*Plate 1038. Serving dish, 6" wide, red mark #27. $60.00–75.00.*

*Plate 1039. Serving dish, 6" wide, green mark #27. $225.00–250.00.*

177

*Plate 1040. Serving dish, 7¼" wide, red mark #27. $225.00–250.00.*

*Plate 1041. Divided serving dish, 9" wide, red mark #27. $55.00–70.00.*

*Plate 1042. Celery dish, 11½" long, red mark #27. $45.00–60.00.*

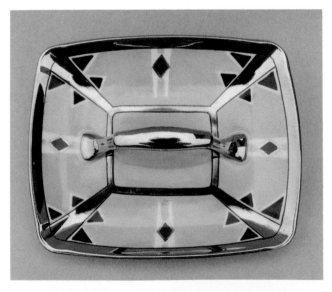

*Plate 1043. Serving tray, 7" long, red mark #27. $70.00–90.00.*

*Plate 1044. Sandwich plate, 7½" wide, red mark #27. $60.00–80.00.*

Plate 1045. Divided serving dish, 8¾" wide, green mark #27. $55.00–70.00.

Plate 1046. Serving tray, 9" wide, red mark #32. $50.00–60.00.

Plate 1047. Relish dish, 8½" long, green mark #27. $25.00–35.00.

Plate 1048. Serving tray, 9" wide, green mark #27. $40.00–50.00.

Plate 1049. Dish, 5" wide, red mark #27. $180.00–210.00.

179

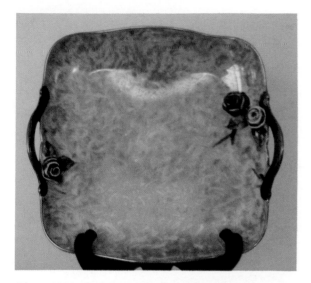

Plate 1050. Serving tray, 9" wide, red mark #27.
$50.00–60.00.

Plate 1051. Chip and dip set, 11½" wide, red mark #27.
$70.00–80.00.

Plate 1052. Sandwich tray, 17½" long, red mark #27. $45.00–60.00.

Plate 1053. Chip and dip dish, 9" wide, green mark #27.
$70.00–80.00.

Plate 1054. Chip and dip dish, 9" wide, green mark #38. $70.00–80.00.

*Plate 1055. Relish dish, 7½" long, red mark #27. $25.00–35.00.*

*Plate 1056. Relish dish, 7" long, green mark #27. $25.00–35.00.*

*Plate 1057. Wall pocket, 8" long, red mark #27. $150.00–175.00.*

*Plate 1059. Relish dish, 8½" long, red mark #27. $25.00–35.00.*

*Plate 1058. Celery dish, 10½" long, red mark #27. $25.00–40.00.*

Plate 1060. Relish dish, 8½" long, red mark #27. $35.00–50.00.

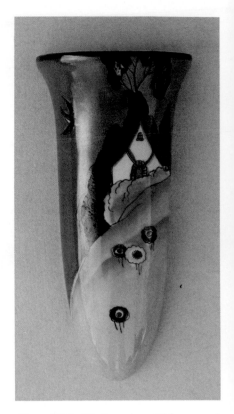

Plate 1061. Wall pocket, 6" long, red mark #27. $110.00–125.00.

Plate 1062. Relish dish, 8¼" long, two compartments lift out, red mark #27. $45.00–60.00.

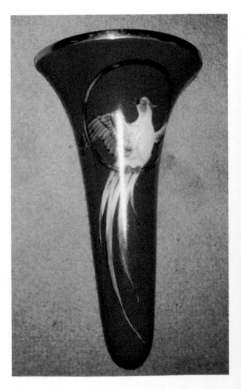

Plate 1064. Wall pocket, 8" tall, green mark #27. $115.00–130.00.

Plate 1063. Bread tray, 12½" long, green mark #27. $35.00–50.00.

Plate 1065. Compote/comport, 6½" wide, green mark #27. $250.00–275.00.

Plate 1067. Compote/comport, 7" wide, green mark #27. $45.00–60.00.

Plate 1068. Compote/comport, 6½" wide, green mark #27. $250.00–275.00.

Plate 1066. Wall pocket, 8" tall, red mark #27. $85.00–105.00.

Plate 1069. Wall pocket, 8" tall, red mark #27. $85.00–105.00.

Plate 1070. Compote/comport, 8½" wide, red mark #27. $60.00–75.00.

Plate 1072. Compote/comport, 4¾" wide, red mark #27. $55.00–65.00.

Plate 1071. Wall pocket, 8" long, green mark #27. $125.00–150.00.

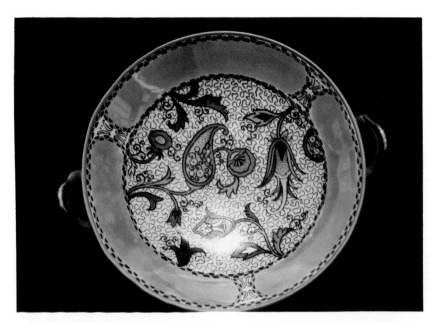

Plate 1073. Compote/comport, 8¼" wide, red mark #27. $60.00–75.00.

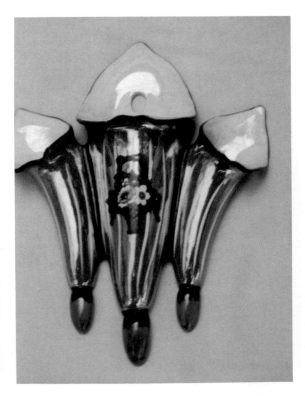

Plate 1074. Wall pocket, green mark #27. $195.00–215.00.

Plate 1075. Compote/comport, 6½" wide, green mark #27. $250.00–275.00.

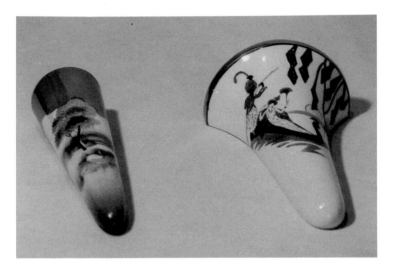

Plate 1076. Wall pockets, each is 8" long, red mark #27. Left, 70.00–85.00; right, 115.00–130.00.

Plate 1077. Wall pocket, 8" long, red mark #27. $135.00–160.00.

Plate 1078. Compote/comport, 11½" wide, green mark #27. $140.00–165.00.

Plate 1079. Compote/comport, 6½" wide, green mark #27. $60.00–75.00.

185

Plate 1080. Compote/comport, 6½" wide, green mark #27. $250.00–275.00.

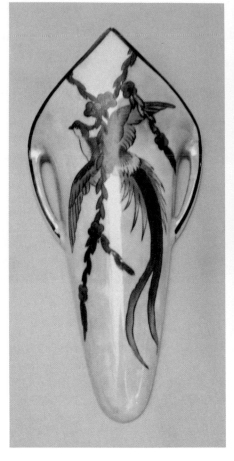

Plate 1081. Wall pocket, 9" long, red mark #27. $110.00–125.00.

Plate 1082. Compote/comport, 10½" wide, red mark #27. $70.00–85.00.

Plate 1083. Compote/comport, 5¾" wide excluding handles, red mark #27. $70.00–85.00.

Plate 1084. Wall pocket, 8" long, red mark #27. $75.00–90.00.

186

*Plate 1085. Compote/comport, 7" wide, red mark #27. $95.00–115.00.*

*Plate 1087. Compote/comport, 9" wide, red mark #27. $70.00–85.00.*

*Plate 1088. Compote/comport, 6" wide, red mark #27. $75.00–90.00.*

*Plate 1086. Wall pocket, 9" long, red mark #27. $95.00–105.00.*

*Plate 1089. Wall pocket, 8" long, red mark #27. $85.00–100.00.*

187

Plate 1090. Compote/comport, 8½" wide, green mark #27. $95.00–115.00.

Plate 1092. Compote/comport, 7" wide, green mark #27. $50.00–65.00.

Plate 1091. Wall pocket, 7" long, red mark #27. $125.00–150.00.

Plate 1093. Compote/comport, 9¾" wide, red mark #27. $65.00–75.00.

Plate 1094. Wall pocket, 8" long, red mark #27. $125.00–140.00.

188

Plate 1095. Compote/comport, 10½" wide, red mark #27. $85.00–100.00.

Plate 1096. Wall pockets, 7" long, red mark #27. $150.00–160.00 pair.

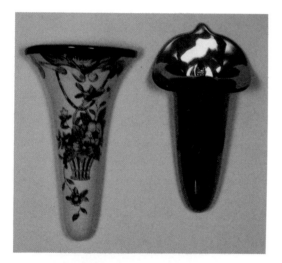

Plate 1097. Wall pockets, 8" long, red mark #27. $75.00–95.00 each.

Plate 1098. Compote/comport, 9½" wide, green mark #27. $95.00–125.00.

Plate 1099. Compote/comport, 10" wide, green mark #27. $80.00–100.00.

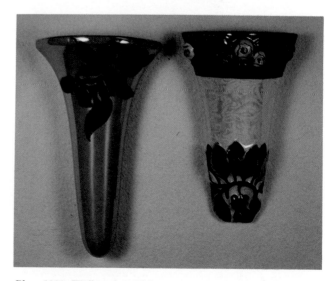

Plate 1100. Wall pocket, 8" long, green mark #27. Wall pocket, 7¼" long, relief molded, red mark #27. Left, $75.00–90.00; right, $175.00–195.00.

Plate 1101. Compote/comport, 5¾" wide, red mark #27. $75.00–90.00.

Plate 1102. Refreshment set, plate, 8½" long, green mark #27. $75.00–95.00 each.

Plate 1103. Breakfast set, tray, 12" long, red mark #27. $90.00–105.00.

Plate 1105. Wall pocket, 8¾" long, green mark #27. $105.00–120.00.

Plate 1104. Wall pocket, 8" long, red mark #27. Wall pocket, 6½" long, green mark #27. Left, 90.00–100.00; right, 115.00–125.00.

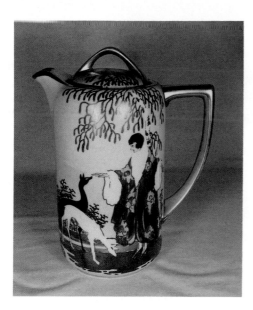

Plate 1106. Chocolate pot, 8¼" tall, green mark #27. $175.00–225.00.

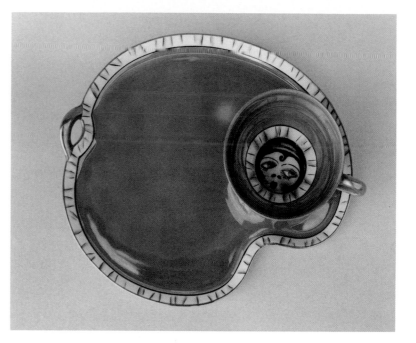

Plate 1107. Refreshment set, plate, 8½" long, green mark #27. $75.00–95.00.

Plate 1108. Refreshment set with punch cups, plate, 8¼" long, green mark #27. $60.00–75.00.

Plate 1109. Ashtray, 4½" wide, green mark #27. $45.00–60.00.

Plate 1110. Refreshment set, plate, 8½" long, green mark #27. $100.00–115.00.

Plate 1111. Teapot, 4" tall, green mark #27. $75.00–85.00.

Plate 1112. Chocolate pot, 8½" tall, green mark #27. $75.00–90.00.

Plate 1113. Chocolate set, pot, 8¼" tall, green mark #27. $250.00–275.00.

Plate 1114. Tea set, teapot, 6½" wide, red mark #27. $100.00–125.00.

Plate 1115. Ashtray, 3" wide, green mark #27. $45.00–55.00.

Plate 1116. Demitasse set, tray, 11" wide, pot, 6¾" tall, comes with 6 cups & saucers, green mark #27. $250.00–300.00.

Plate 1117. Chocolate pot, 9¾" tall, green mark #27. $75.00–85.00.

Plate 1118. Humidor, 6½" tall, green mark #27. $375.00–400.00.

Plate 1119. Demitasse set, green mark #27. $275.00–300.00.

Plate 1120. Cigarette holder/playing card holder, 3" tall, red mark #27. $85.00–110.00.

Plate 1121. Tea set, pot, 5½" tall, green mark #27. $135.00–160.00.

Plate 1122. Humidor, 7¾" tall, green mark #27. $340.00–380.00.

Plate 1123. Demitasse set, red mark #27. $200.00–240.00.

Plate 1124. Demitasse set, tray 12" wide, red mark #27. $400.00–450.00.

Plate 1125. Humidor, 6" tall, green mark #27. $195.00–230.00.

Plate 1126. Tea set, green mark #27. $295.00–325.00.

Plate 1127. Humidor, 5" tall, red mark #27. $185.00–210.00.

Plate 1128. Demitasse set, red mark #27. $250.00–275.00.

Plate 1129. Humidor, 6" tall, green mark #27. $275.00–325.00.

Plate 1130. Tea set, comes with four cups, saucers and plates, plates are 7½" wide, red mark #27. $325.00–350.00.

Plate 1132. Teapot, 5" tall, green mark #27. $65.00–75.00.

Plate 1131. Humidor, 5½" tall, green mark #27. $165.00–190.00.

Plate 1133. Teapot, 4½" tall, green mark #27. $65.00–75.00.

Plate 1134. Coffee set, pot, 7¼" tall, green mark #27. $175.00–200.00.

Plate 1135. Tea set, comes with six cups and saucers, green mark #27. $275.00–300.00.

Plate 1136. Ashtray, 5" wide, red mark #27. $55.00–70.00.

Plate 1137. Ashtray, 5" wide, green mark #27. $60.00–80.00.

Plate 1138. Tea set, red mark #27. $295.00–325.00.

Plate 1139. Match holder, 2¾" tall, red mark #27. $60.00–75.00.

Plate 1140. Tea set, green mark #27. $295.00–325.00.

Plate 1141. Ashtray, 4¼" wide, red mark #27. $65.00–75.00.

Plate 1142. Humidor, 6½" tall, green mark #27. $185.00–205.00.

Plate 1143. Cup and saucer sets, red mark #27. $40.00–55.00 each set.

Plate 1144. Children's tea set, teapot, 3½" tall, red mark #27. $135.00–150.00.

Plate 1145. Ashtray, 5" wide, red mark #27. $195.00–210.00.

Plate 1146. Humidor, 6½" tall, green mark #27. $185.00–220.00.

Plate 1147. Humidor, 5¾" tall, green mark #27. $225.00–260.00.

Plate 1148. Ashtray, red mark #27. $135.00–150.00.

Plate 1149. Ashtray, 5" wide, green mark #27. $195.00–210.00.

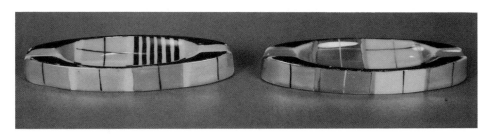

Plate 1150. Ashtrays, each 4¼" long, red mark #27. $50.00–65.00 pair.

Plate 1051. Cigarette box, 3½" long, green mark #27. $100.00–120.00.

Plate 1152. Ashtray, 4" wide, red mark #27. $120.00–140.00.

Plate 1153. Ashtray, 4" wide, green mark #27. $75.00–95.00.

Plate 1154. *Smoke set, tray, 6½" long, red mark #27.*
*$225.00–250.00.*

Plate 1155. *Ashtray, 3½" wide, green mark*
*#27. $45.00–55.00.*

Plate 1156. *Cigarette holder/playing card holder,*
*3" tall, red mark #27. $150.00–175.00.*

Plate 1157. *Cigarette holder/playing card*
*holder, 4" tall, red mark #27. $150.00–175.00.*

Plate 1158. *Cigarette holder/playing card holder,*
*3¾" tall, red mark #27. $160.00–185.00.*

Plate 1159. *Ashtray & match holder, 3" tall, red*
*mark #27. $150.00–180.00.*

199

Plate 1160. Cigarette holder/playing card holders, 3¾" tall, red mark #27. Left, $60.00–75.00; right, $95.00–110.00.

Plate 1161. Cigarette holder/playing card holder, 3¾" tall, red mark #27. $95.00–110.00.

Plate 1162. Ashtray, 3¾" long, red mark #27. $85.00–95.00.

Plate 1163. Cigarette holder/playing card holder, 4½" tall, green mark #27. $115.00–125.00.

Plate 1164. Smoke set, tray, 7¾" long, red mark #27. $45.00–55.00.

Plate 1165. Match holder, red mark #27. $115.00–130.00.

Plate 1166. Cigarette holder, red mark #27. $115.00–130.00.

Plate 1167. Cigarette box, 3½" long, red mark #27. $175.00–195.00.

Plate 1168. Ashtray, 5½" wide, green mark #27. $55.00–65.00.

Plate 1169. Cigarette box, 3¾" long, red mark #27. $225.00–250.00.

Plate 1170. Smoke set, tray, 7" long, red mark #27. $225.00–250.00.

Plate 1171. Smoke set, tray, 7" long, green mark #27. $125.00–150.00.

Plate 1172. Cigarette box, 3¾" long, red mark #27. $225.00–250.00.

Plate 1173. Cigarette box, 3¾" wide, red mark #27. $225.00–250.00.

Plate 1174. Smoke set, tray, 7" long, green mark #27. $250.00–285.00.

Plate 1175. Cigarette holder/playing card holder, 3¾" tall, green mark #27. $95.00–110.00.

Plate 1176. Smoke set, tray, 7" long, red mark #27. $225.00–250.00.

Plate 1177. Cigarette holders/playing card holders, 3¾" tall, red mark #27. Left, $175.00–200.00; right, $110.00–130.00.

Plate 1178. Ashtray & match holder, 2" tall, red mark #27. $200.00–230.00.

Plate 1179. Ashtray & match holder, red mark #27. $200.00–230.00.

*Plate 1180. Cruet set, 8" long, red mark #27. $85.00–100.00.*

*Plate 1181. Cruet set, 6¾" tall, red mark #27. $60.00–80.00.*

*Plate 1182. Cruet set, 6½" wide, red mark #27. $60.00–80.00.*

*Plate 1183. Cruet set, tray, 8" long, red mark #27. $65.00–85.00.*

*Plate 1184. Perfume bottle, 6" tall,
red mark #27. $175.00–200.00.*

Plate 1185. Cologne bottle, 6¾" tall, red mark #27. $175.00–200.00.

Plate 1186. Trinket box, 3½" wide, red mark #27. $225.00–260.00.

Plate 1187. Powder box & hair receiver, 3½" wide, green mark #27. $100.00–140.00 set.

Plate 1188. Cologne bottle, 6½" tall, red mark #27; powder puff box, 4" wide, red mark #27. $125.00–150.00 each.

Plate 1189. Perfume bottle with original box, 6" tall, red mark #27. $150.00–170.00.

Plate 1190. Trinket dish, 3½" wide, red mark #27. $65.00–75.00.

Plate 1191. Cologne bottle, 6¾" tall, red mark #27. $175.00–200.00.

Plate 1193. Perfume bottle, 6" tall, red mark #27. $175.00–200.00.

Plate 1192. Cologne bottle, 6¾" tall, red mark #27. $150.00–175.00.

Plate 1194. Footed trinket box, 4" wide, red mark #27. $35.00–45.00.

Plate 1195. Perfume bottle,
6" tall, red mark #27.
$125.00–150.00.

Plate 1196. Dresser tray, 8½" long, red mark #27. $225.00–250.00.

Plate 1197. Rouge box, 2½" wide, red
mark #27. $195.00–215.00.

Plate 1198. Dresser tray, 8½" long, red mark #27. $225.00–250.00.

Plate 1199. Powder puff box, 3¼" wide, green
mark #27. $210.00–235.00.

Plate 1200. Powder box, 4¾" wide, red mark #27. $55.00–65.00.

*Plate 1201. Dresser tray, 11" long, red mark #27. $250.00–300.00.*

*Plate 1202. Trinket dish, 3½" wide, red mark #27, $25.00–35.00.*

*Plate 1203. Powder puff box, 4" wide, green mark #27. Powder puff box, 4" wide, red mark #27. Left, $175.00–200.00; right, $160.00–175.00.*

*Plate 1204. Powder puff box, 3½" wide, red mark #27. $160.00–175.00.*

*Plate 1206. Dresser tray, 10½" long, green mark #27. $225.00–250.00.*

*Plate 1205. Powder puff box, 4" wide, green mark #27. $160.00–175.00.*

Plate 1207. Dresser tray, 8½" long, red mark #27. $215.00–235.00.

Plate 1208. Powder puff box, 3½" wide, red mark #27. $160.00–175.00.

Plate 1209. Powder puff boxes. Left, $250.00–275.00; right, 225.00–250.00.

Plate 1210. Powder puff box, 4" wide, red mark #27. $175.00–195.00.

Plate 1211. Dresser tray, 8½" long, red mark #27. $215.00–235.00.

Plate 1212. Powder puff box, 3½" wide, red mark #27. $175.00–195.00.

Plate 1213. Powder puff box, 4" wide, red mark #27. $160.00–175.00.

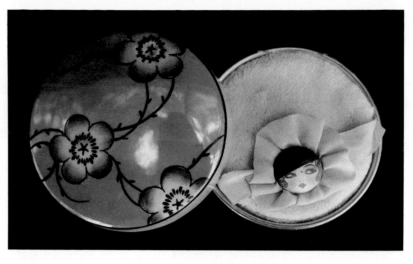

Plate 1214. Powder puff box, 4" wide, green mark #27. $200.00–225.00.

Plate 1215. Powder puff box, 3½" wide, red mark #27. $200.00–225.00.

Plate 1216. Powder puff box, 3¾" wide, red mark #27. $140.00–155.00.

Plate 1217. Dresser tray, 11" long, red mark #27. $50.00–65.00.

Plate 1218. Powder puff box, 4" wide, red mark #27. $160.00–175.00.

Plate 1219. Dresser tray, 8" wide. Powder box, 3" wide, red mark #27. $275.00–320.00.

Plate 1220. Powder puff box, 3½" wide, green mark #27. $200.00–225.00.

Plate 1221. Powder puff box, 4¾" wide, red mark #27. $175.00–195.00.

Plate 1222. Powder puff box, 4" wide, red mark #27. $225.00–250.00.

*Plate 1223. Powder puff box, 4" wide, red mark #27. $175.00–195.00.*

*Plate 1224. Powder puff box, 4" wide, red mark #27. $200.00–225.00.*

*Plate 1225. Powder puff box, 3½" wide, red mark #27. $195.00–215.00.*

*Plate 1226. Powder puff box, 4" wide, green mark #27. $175.00–195.00.*

*Plate 1227. Powder puff box, 3½" wide, red mark #27. $175.00–195.00.*

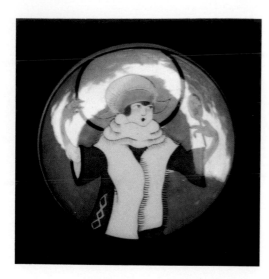

Plate 1228. Powder puff box, 3½" wide, red mark #27. $175.00–195.00.

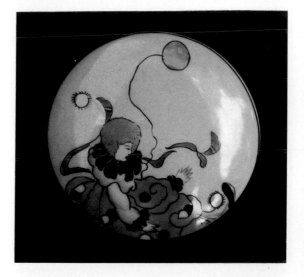

Plate 1229. Powder puff box, 4" wide, green mark #27. $175.00–195.00.

Plate 1230. Cosmetic jar, 2½" wide, green mark #27. $140.00–160.00.

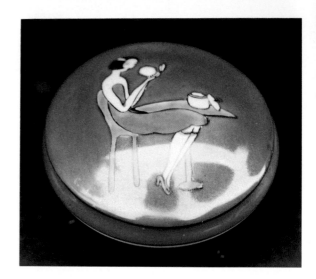

Plate 1231. Footed trinket box, 3" wide, green mark #27. $120.00–140.00.

Plate 1232. Powder puff box, 3¼" wide, red mark #27. $175.00–195.00.

Plate 1233. Powder puff box, 3¼" wide, red mark #27. $160.00–175.00.

Plate 1234. Powder puff box, 4" wide, green mark #27. $175.00–195.00.

Plate 1235. Powder puff box, 4" wide, green mark #27. $175.00–195.00.

Plate 1236. Powder puff box, 4" wide, red mark #27. $160.00–180.00.

Plate 1237. Powder puff box, 3½" wide, green mark #27. $140.00–160.00.

Plate 1238. Powder puff box, 4" wide, green mark #27. $200.00–225.00.

Plate 1239. Powder puff box, 4" wide, red mark #27. $200.00–225.00.

Plate 1241. Cake plate, 9¾" wide, red mark #27. $65.00–80.00.

Plate 1240. Cake plate, 10½" wide, green mark #27. $65.00–80.00.

Plate 1243. Cake plate, 9½" wide, green mark #27. $55.00–65.00.

Plate 1242. Cake plate, 10½" wide, green mark #27. $75.00–95.00.

Plate 1244. Cake plate, 9¾" wide, red mark #27. $65.00–75.00.

Plate 1245. Cake plate, 10¼" wide, red mark #27. $65.00–75.00.

Plate 1246. Cake plate, 9¾" wide, red mark #27. $55.00–65.00.

Plate 1247. Cake plate, 9¾" wide, red mark #29. $95.00–115.00.

Plate 1248. Cake plate, 9¾" wide, green mark #27. $45.00–55.00.

Plate 1249. Cake plate, 10½" wide, red mark #27. $45.00–55.00.

Plate 1250. Pedestalled cake plate, 10½" wide, red mark #27. $45.00–55.00.

Plate 1251. Cake plate, 9½" wide, green mark #27. $45.00–55.00.

Plate 1252. Cake plate, 10½" wide, red mark #27. $45.00–55.00.

Plate 1253. Cake plate, 9" wide, red mark #27. $60.00–70.00.

Plate 1254. Cake plate, 9¾" wide, green mark #27. $60.00–70.00.

Plate 1255. Cake plate, 9½" wide, red mark #27. $75.00–95.00.

Plate 1256. Cake plate, 9½" wide, red mark #27. $35.00–45.00.

Plate 1258. Cake plate, 9½" wide, green mark #27. $55.00–65.00.

Plate 1257. Cake plate, 9½" wide, red mark #27. $45.00–55.00.

Plate 1260. Cake plate, 10¼" wide, red mark #27. $75.00–85.00.

Plate 1259. Cake plate, 10" wide, red mark #27. $55.00–65.00.

Plate 1261. Cake plate, 10" wide, red mark #27. $45.00–55.00.

Plate 1262. Cake plate, 10½" wide, green mark #27. $145.00–160.00.

Plate 1263. Cake plate, 9¼" wide, green mark #37. $45.00–55.00.

Plate 1264. Cake plate, 9½" wide, green mark #27. $45.00–55.00.

Plate 1266. Cake plate, 9¾" wide, red mark #27. $35.00–45.00.

Plate 1265. Cake plate, 9½" wide, green mark #27. $35.00–45.00.

Plate 1268. Cake plate, 9½" wide, green mark #27. $35.00–45.00.

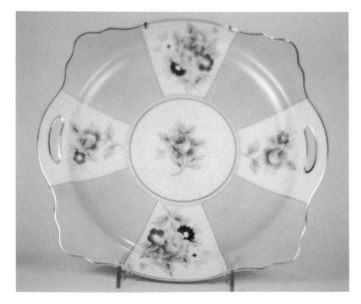

Plate 1267. Cake plate, 10" wide, red mark #27. $35.00–45.00.

*Plate 1269. Cake plate, 9¾" wide, green mark #27. $35.00–45.00.*

*Plate 1270. Individual size cake plates, matches plate 1269. 6½" wide, green mark #27. $15.00–20.00.*

*Plate 1271. Cake plate, 10¼" wide, red mark #27. $35.00–45.00.*

*Plate 1272. Cake plate, 9½" wide, green mark #27. $35.00–45.00.*

Plate 1274. Pedestalled cake plate, 10½" wide, red mark #27. $40.00–50.00.

Plate 1273. Cake plate 9½" wide, red mark #27. Similar to plate 1256. $35.00–45.00.

Plate 1276. Cake set, large plate, 9½" wide, small plate, 6" wide, set comes with six small plates, red mark #27. $100.00–130.00 set.

Plate 1275. Cake plate, 9½" wide, red mark #27. $35.00–45.00.

Plate 1277. Cake plate, 10¼" wide, green mark #27. $150.00–180.00.

Plate 1278. Plate, 7½" wide, red mark #27. $15.00–20.00.

Plate 1279. Plate, 6¼" wide, red mark #27. $15.00–20.00.

Plate 1280. Individual size cake plate, matches plate 1277, 7½" wide, green mark #27. $25.00–30.00.

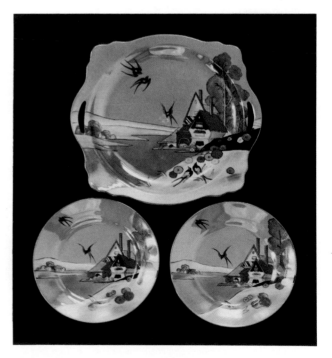

Plate 1281. Cake set, cake plate, 10" wide, individual plates, 6½" wide, green mark #27. $115.00–130.00 set.

Plate 1282. Cake plate, 10" wide, green mark #27. $165.00–185.00.

Plate 1283. Plate, 6½" wide, green mark #27. $15.00–20.00.

Plate 1284. Plate, 6¼" wide, green mark #27. $15.00–20.00.

Plate 1285. Cake plate, 10½" wide, red mark #27. $75.00–90.00.

Plate 1286. Plate, 6¼" wide, red mark #27. $15.00–20.00.

Plate 1287. Cake plate, 10" wide, red mark #27. $55.00–65.00.

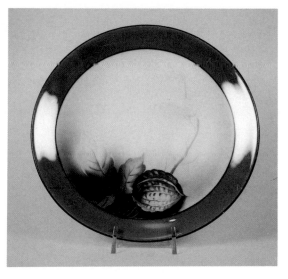

Plate 1288. Plate, 7¾" wide, red mark #27. $15.00–20.00.

Plate 1289. Plate, 7¾" wide, green mark #27. $15.00–20.00.

Plate 1290. Cake plate, 11" wide, red mark #27. $60.00–70.00.

Plate 1291. Plate, 7½" wide, red mark #27. $15.00–20.00.

Plate 1292. Cake set, cake plate, 10¼" wide, small plates, 6¼" wide, set has 6 plates, red mark #27. $275.00–300.00 set.

Plate 1293. Bread set, large plate, 7¾" wide, small butter pats, 3¾" wide, green mark #27. $85.00–95.00.

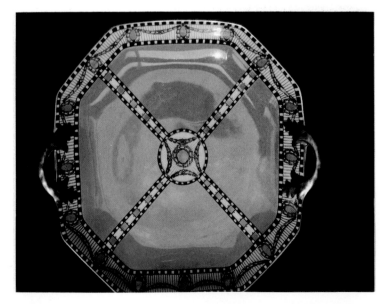

Plate 1294. Cake plate, 11" wide, green mark #27. $40.00–50.00.

Plate 1295. Plate, 7¾" wide, red mark #27. $15.00–20.00.

Plate 1296. Cake set, cake plate, 12" wide, small plates, 6" wide, set comes with 6 plates, green mark #27. $100.00–140.00 set.

Plate 1297. Plate, 8½" wide, red mark #27. $215.00–235.00.

Plate 1298. Plate, 6¼" wide, green mark #27. $85.00–95.00.

Plate 1299. Plate, 7" wide, red mark #27. $120.00–135.00.

Plate 1300. Plate, 8½" wide, green mark #27. $60.00–70.00.

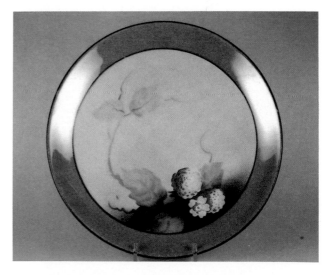

Plate 1301. Plate, 7½" wide, red mark #27. $20.00–30.00.

227

*Plate 1302. Plate, 6¼" wide, artist signed F. Honda, green mark #27. $20.00–30.00.*

*Plate 1303. Plate, 6¼" wide, artist signed F. Honda, green mark #27. $20.00–30.00.*

*Plate 1304. Plates, 6¼" wide, red mark #27. $235.00–255.00 each.*

*Plate 1305. Plate, 7¾" wide, red mark #27. $20.00–30.00.*

*Plate 1306. Plate, 5¾" wide, green mark #27. $20.00–30.00.*

Plate 1307. Plate, 7¾" wide, artist signed F. Honda, green mark #27. $20.00–30.00.

Plate 1308. Plate, 5¾" wide, green mark #27. $20.00–30.00.

Plate 1309. Wall plaque, 7½" wide, green mark #27. $215.00–235.00.

Plate 1310. Plate, 8" wide, green mark #27. $20.00–30.00.

Plate 1311. Plate, 6½" wide, green mark #38. $20.00–30.00.

Plate 1312. Plate, 7¾" wide, red mark #27. $20.00–30.00.

Plate 1313. Plate, 7½" wide, green mark #27. $20.00–30.00.

Plate 1314. Plate, 8½" wide, red mark #27. $20.00–30.00.

Plate 1315. Plate, 6¼" wide, artist signed, F. Honda, green mark #27. $20.00–30.00.

*Plate 1316. Plate, 7¾" wide, green mark #27. $20.00–30.00.*

*Plate 1317. Plate, 7¾" wide, green mark #27. $20.00–30.00.*

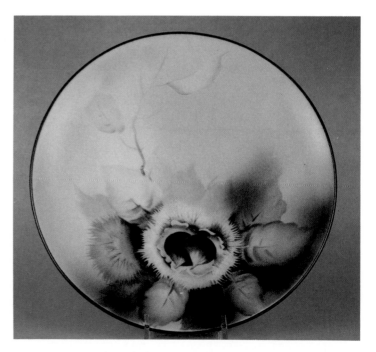

*Plate 1318. Plate, 7¾" wide, green mark #27. $20.00–30.00.*

*Plate 1319. Plate, 7¾" wide, green mark #27. $20.00–30.00.*

Plate 1321. Plate, 7¼" wide, red mark #27. $20.00–30.00.

Plate 1320. Plate, 7¾" wide, green mark #27. $20.00–30.00.

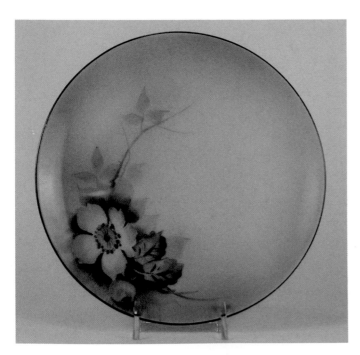

Plate 1323. Plate, 7¾" wide, green mark #27. $40.00–50.00.

Plate 1322. Plate, 6½" wide, red mark #27. $20.00–30.00.

Plate 1324. Plate, 8½" wide, green mark #27. $40.00–50.00.

Plate 1325. Plate, 7½" wide, green mark #27. $40.00–50.00.

Plate 1326. Plate, 7¾" wide, red mark #27. $40.00–50.00.

Plate 1327. Plate, 8½" wide, green mark #27. $40.00–50.00.

Plate 1328. Plate, 7¾" wide, green mark #27. $20.00–30.00.

Plate 1329. Plate, 7¾" wide, red mark #27. $25.00–35.00.

Plate 1330. Wall plaque, 8¾" wide, green mark #27. $135.00–155.00.

Plate 1331. Plate, 7½" wide, green mark #38. $15.00–25.00.

Plate 1332. Plate, 6¼" wide, green mark #27. $30.00–40.00.

Plate 1333. Plate, 7¾" wide, green mark #27. $30.00–40.00.

Plate 1334. Plate, 6¼" wide, green mark #27. $30.00–40.00.

Plate 1335. Plate, 6¼" wide, green mark #27. $30.00–40.00.

*Plate 1336. Plate, 7¾" wide, green mark #27. $30.00–40.00.*

*Plate 1337. Plate, 7¾" wide, green mark #27. $30.00–40.00.*

*Plate 1338. Plate, 7¾" wide, green mark #27. $30.00–40.00.*

*Plate 1339. Plate, 7¾" wide, green mark #27. $30.00–40.00.*

Plate 1340. Plate, 7¾" wide, green mark #27.
$30.00–40.00.

Plate 1341. Plate, 7¾" wide, green mark #27.
$30.00–40.00.

Plate 1342. Plate, 6½" wide, green mark #27.
$15.00–25.00.

Plate 1343. Plate, 7¾" wide, green mark #27. $30.00–40.00.

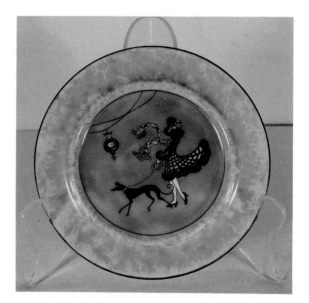

Plate 1344. Plate, 6½" wide, red mark #27.
$145.00–175.00.

*Plate 1346. Plate, 6¼" wide, red mark #27. $195.00–215.00.*

*Plate 1345. Wall plaque, 7¾" wide, green mark #27. $195.00–215.00.*

*Plate 1348. Plate 8½" wide, red mark #27. $215.00–235.00.*

*Plate 1347. Plate, 7¾" wide, red mark #27. $195.00–215.00.*

*Plate 1349. Plate, 7¾" wide, red mark #27. $195.00–215.00.*

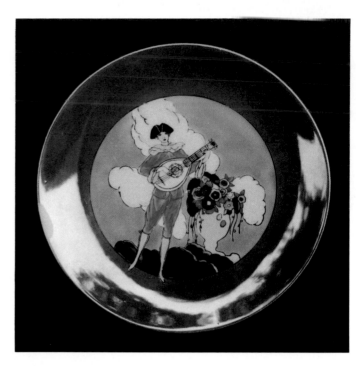

*Plate 1350. Plate, 7¾" wide, red mark #27. $195.00–215.00.*

*Plate 1351. Plate, 8¾" wide, red mark #27. $215.00–230.00.*

*Plate 1352. Plate, 7¾" wide, red mark #27. $195.00–215.00.*

**Plate 1353.** *Plate, 6¾" wide, red mark #27.*
*$195.00–215.00.*

**Plate 1354.** *Plate, 8½" wide, red mark #27.*
*$215.00–230.00.*

**Plate 1355.** *Plate, 7¾" wide, green mark*
*#27. $195.00–215.00.*

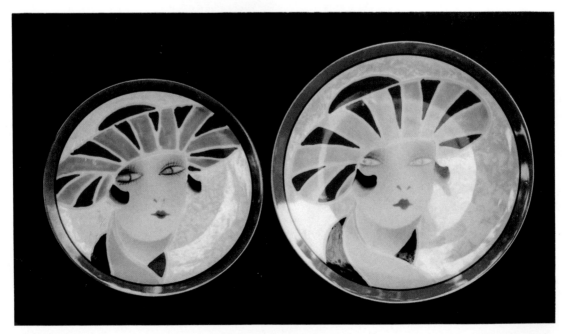

**Plate 1356.** *Plate, 6¼" wide, red mark #27. Plate, 7½" wide, red mark #27. Left, 175.00–195.00; right,*
*195.00–210.00.*

Plate 1357. Plate, 9" wide, red mark #27. $275.00–300.00.

Plate 1358. Plate, 9" wide, red mark #34. $275.00–300.00.

Plate 1359. Plate, 9" wide, green mark #27. $275.00–300.00.

Plate 1360. Plate, 9" wide, green mark #27. $275.00–300.00.

Plate 1361. Wall plaque, 8½" wide, green mark #27. $215.00–235.00.

Plate 1362. Vase, 6¼" tall, green mark #27. $75.00–90.00.

Plate 1363. Wall plaque, 8½" wide, green mark #27. $215.00–235.00.

Plate 1364. Vase, 8" tall, green mark #27. $110.00–130.00.

Plate 1365. Vase, 6" tall, red mark
#27. $140.00–160.00.

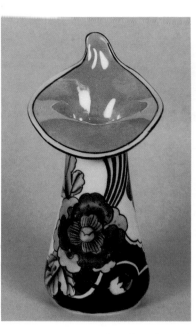

Plate 1366. Vase, 6¾" tall, red mark
#27. $145.00–165.00.

Plate 1367. Vase, 8½" tall, red mark #27. Vase, 7½" tall,
red mark #27. Left, $135.00–150.00; right,
$145.00–165.00.

Plate 1368. Vase, 8¾" tall, red
mark #27. $85.00–100.00.

Plate 1369. Vase, 7¼" tall, green
mark #27. $95.00–110.00.

Plate 1370. Vase, 6" tall, red mark #27. $95.00–110.00.

243

Plate 1371. Vase, 6½" tall, green mark #27. $70.00–80.00.

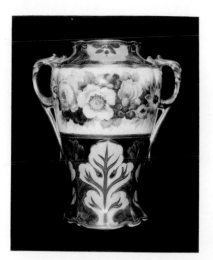

Plate 1372. Vase, 9" tall, green mark #27. $85.00–100.00.

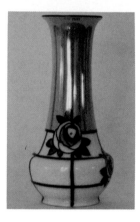

Plate 1374. Vase, 5¾" tall, green mark #27. $55.00–65.00.

Plate 1376. Vase, 6" tall, red mark #27. $70.00–80.00.

Plate 1373. Vase, 6" tall, green mark #27. $70.00–80.00.

Plate 1375. Vase, 7" tall, red mark #27. $95.00–110.00.

Plate 1377. Vase, 7½" tall, green mark #27. $85.00–95.00.

Plate 1378. Vase, 7" tall, red mark #50. $85.00–100.00.

Plate 1379. Vase, 8¾" tall, red mark #27. $80.00–95.00.

Plate 1380. Vase, 8" tall, red mark #52. $70.00–80.00.

Plate 1381. Vase, 10½" tall, green mark #27. $90.00–105.00.

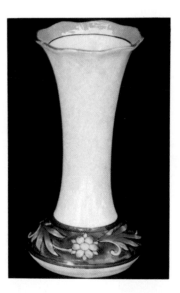

Plate 1382. Vase, 6" tall, green mark #27. $55.00–70.00.

Plate 1383. Vase, 6¾" tall, red mark #27. $60.00–75.00.

Plate 1384. Basket vase, 10" tall, red mark #27. $200.00–230.00.

Plate 1385. Basket vase, 10" tall, red mark #27. $200.00–230.00.

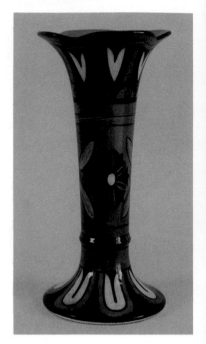

Plate 1386. Vase, 8" tall, green mark #27. $75.00–85.00.

Plate 1387. Basket vase, 10" tall, red mark #27. $300.00–340.00.

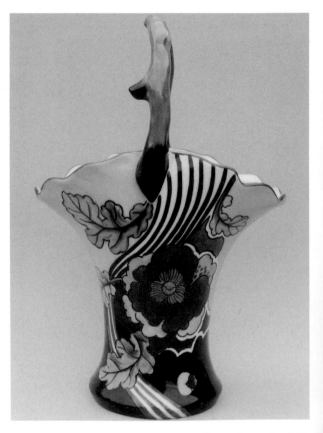

Plate 1388. Basket vase, 10" tall, red mark #27. $200.00–230.00.

Plate 1389. Basket vase, 6¼" tall, green mark #27. $120.00–135.00.

Plate 1390. Basket vase, 7½" tall, red mark #27. $120.00–135.00.

Plate 1392. Vase, 7½" tall, green mark #27. $85.00–95.00.

Plate 1393. Vase, 5¼" tall, red mark #27. $60.00–75.00.

Plate 1391. Vase, 6½" tall, red mark #27. $85.00–95.00.

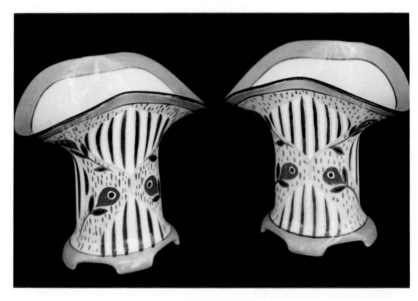

Plate 1394. Pair of vases, 6½" tall, red mark #27. $150.00–160.00 pair.

Plate 1395. Basket vase, 6" tall, red mark #27. $85.00–95.00.

Plate 1396. Vase, 7" tall, red mark #27. $60.00–75.00.

Plate 1397. Vase, 10" tall, green mark #27. $95.00–110.00.

Plate 1398. Vase, 5¾" tall, red mark #27. $75.00–90.00.

Plate 1399. Vase, 7" tall, red mark #27. $80.00–95.00.

Plate 1400. Vase, 7½" tall, red mark #27. $110.00–125.00.

Plate 1401. Vase, 8" tall, red mark #27. $135.00–150.00.

Plate 1402. Basket vase, 8" tall, green mark #27. $135.00–150.00.

Plate 1403. Vase, 7½" tall, green
mark #27. $95.00–110.00.

Plate 1404. Vase, 5½" tall, red mark #27. $70.00–85.00.

Plate 1406. Vase with flower frog, 4½" tall, red mark #27. $125.00–150.00.

Plate 1405. Vase, 6½" tall, red mark
#27. $85.00–95.00.

Plate 1407. Vase, 10¼" tall, green
mark #27. $95.00–110.00.

Plate 1406A. Top view of plate 1406.

Plate 1408. Pair of vases, 8¾" tall, green mark #27. $200.00–240.00 pair.

Plate 1409. Vase, 11" tall, green mark #27. $145.00–160.00.

Plate 1410. Vase, 6¼" tall, red mark #27. $175.00–220.00.

Plate 1411. Vase, 8" tall, red mark #27. $85.00–100.00.

Plate 1412. Vase, 9½" tall, green mark #27. $100.00–120.00.

Plate 1413. Vase, 7" tall, red mark #27. $95.00–110.00.

Plate 1414. Vase, 6" tall, green mark #27. $90.00–105.00.

Plate 1415. Vase, 6¾" tall, red mark #27. Vase, 8" tall, red mark #27. Left, $85.00–95.00; right, $100.00–110.00.

Plate 1416. Basket vase, 6½" tall, red mark #27. $155.00–175.00.

Plate 1417. Vase, 7¼" tall, red mark
#27. $275.00–300.00.

Plate 1418. Vase, 6" tall, green mark #27.
$110.00–125.00.

Plate 1419. Vase, 8½" tall, red mark
#27. $235.00–260.00.

Plate 1420. Vase, 6" tall, green mark #27. Vase, 6" tall, green mark #27.
$85.00–95.00 each.

Plate 1421. Vase, 9½" tall, red
mark #27. $100.00–125.00.

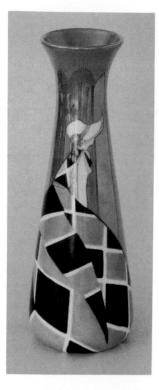

Plate 1422. Vase, 8½" tall, red mark #27. $235.00–260.00.

Plate 1423. Vase, 9" tall, red mark #27. $240.00–270.00.

Plate 1424. Vase, 7¼" tall, red mark #27. $245.00–270.00.

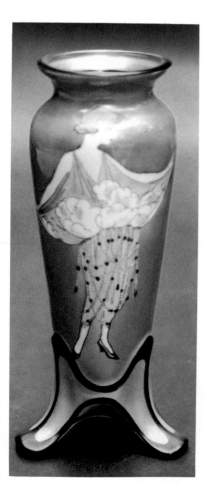

Plate 1425. Vase, 7¼" tall, red mark #27. $225.00–250.00.

Plate 1426. Pair of covered urns, 13" tall, red mark #27. $525.00–575.00 pair.

Plate 1427. Pair of vases, 8½" tall, red mark #27. $250.00–300.00 pair.

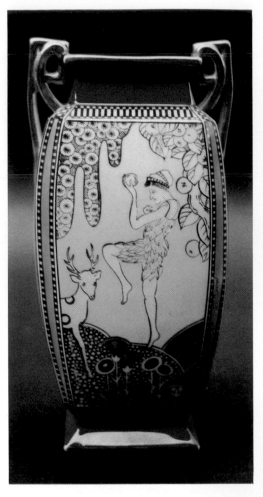

Plate 1428. Vase, 9½" tall, green mark #27. $150.00–180.00.

Plate 1429. Pair of covered urns, 14¼" tall, red mark #27. $325.00–360.00 pair.

Plate 1430. Pair of vases, 8" tall, red mark #27. $325.00–360.00 pair.

# Index
## by Plate Numbers

Mayonnaise set – Plate #'s 895, 902-904, 907, 912, 913.

Mint set – Plate #928.

Mustard jar – Plate #'s 859, 927, 965.

# N – O

Napkin ring – Plate #938.

Nappy (see bowl)

Open salt – Plate #'s 575-577, 881.

# P

Pancake server – Plate #929.

Perfume bottle – Plate #'s 1184, 1189, 1193, 1195.

Pin dish – Plate #'s 486, 489, 491, 492.

Pipe holder – Plate #553.

Pitcher – Plate #'s 970, 972, 974, 976.

Place card holder – Plate #'s 602, 604, 605.

Plate – Plate #'s 1278, 1279, 1283, 1284, 1286, 1288, 1289, 1291, 1295-1308, 1331-1334, 1346-1360.

Playing card holder (see cigarette holder).

Potpourri jar – Plate #'s 984, 986-988.

Powder box – Plate #'s 474, 476, 479, 480, 485, 488, 1187, 1200, 1219.

Powder puff box – Plate #'s 498, 634, 1199, 1203-1205, 1208, 1210, 1212-1216, 1218, 1220, 1221-1229, 1232-1239.

Punch bowl – Plate #'s 1009, 1013.

# R

Refreshment set – Plate #'s 1102, 1107, 1108, 1110.

Relish dish – Plate #'s 599, 600, 1037, 1047, 1055, 1056, 1058, 1060, 1062.

Rouge box – Plate #1197.

# S

Salad bowl – Plate #'s 947, 951, 952, 954.

Salt set – Plate #'s 579, 580, 955.

Salt and pepper set – Plate #'s 572-574, 578, 581, 582, 633, 880, 885, 890, 900.

Sandwich plate/tray – Plate #'s 1020-1026, 1028, 1030, 1033, 1044, 1052.

Sauce dish – Plate #'s 619, 878, 884, 887-888, 891-892, 897, 899, 901, 905-906.

Serving dish – Plate #'s 1029, 1031, 1034, 1035, 1036, 1038-1041, 1043, 1045, 1046, 1048, 1049, 1050.

Slanted cheese – Plate #'s 926, 982.

Smoke set – Plate #'s 1154, 1170-1171, 1174, 1176.

Smoke set tray – Plate #1164.

Spooner – Plate #'s 591, 989-994.

Sugar bowl – Plate #'s 879, 921.

Sugar shaker – Plate #'s 590, 857, 866.

Sweetmeat set – Plate #'s 933.

Syrup – Plate #'s 932, 941, 942.

# T

Teapot – Plate #'s 1111, 1132, 1133.

Tea set – Plate #'s 607, 1114, 1121, 1126, 1130, 1135, 1138, 1140.

Tobacco jar – Plate # 548.

Tray – Plate #609.

Trinket box – Plate #'s 1194, 1231.

Trinket dish – Plate #'s 1186, 1190, 1202.

Trivet/tea tile – Plate #'s 908, 909, 914-917.

# U – W

Urn – Plate #'s 1426, 1429.

Vase – Plate #'s 554-560, 611-614, 626, 629, 638-640, 1362, 1364-1425, 1427, 1428, 1430.

Wall plaque – Plate #'s 636, 1061, 1064, 1309, 1330, 1345, 1361, 1363.

Wall pocket – Plate #'s 529, 532, 583, 584, 615-618, 1057, 1066, 1069, 1071, 1074, 1076, 1077, 1081, 1084, 1086, 1089, 1091, 1094, 1096, 1097, 1100, 1104, 1105.

# Glossary

**Art Deco** – a style of decoration which hit its peak in Europe and America around 1925 although items were manufactured with this decor as early as 1910. The style was modernistic. Geometric patterns were popular. Motifs used were shapes such as circles, rectangles, cylinders, and cones.

**Art Nouveau** – the name is derived from the French words meaning new art. During the period of 1885-1925 artists tended to use bolder colors and realism was rejected. Free-flowing designs were used breaking away from the imitations of the past. Although it lasted until 1925 pattern its popularity waned after 1910.

**Azalea pattern** – pattern found on both Nippon and Noritake marked items. The pattern is one of pink azaleas with green to gray leaves and gold rims. Nippon era pieces match the later Noritake items. This pattern was exclusive with the Larkin Company and was offered to its customers as a premium.

**Backstamp** – mark found on items identifying the manufacturer, exporter or importer, and country of origin.

**Blank** – greenware of bisque items devoid of decoration.

**Blown-out** – this term is used by collectors and dealers for items that have a relief molded pattern embossed on by the mold in which the item was shaped. It is not actually "blown-out" as glass items are but the pattern is raised up from the background of the item. See relief molded.

**Biscuit** – clay which has been fired but unglazed.

**Bisque** – same as biscuit, term also used by collectors to describe a matte finish on an item.

**Casting** – the process of making reproductions by pouring slip into molds.

**Cha no yu** – Japanese tea ceremony.

**Chargers** – archaic term for large platters or plates.

**Cheese hard clay** – same as leather hard clay.

**Cobalt oxide** – blue oxide imported to Japan after 1868 for the decoration of wares. Gosu, a pebble found in Oriental riverbeds had previously been used but was scarce and more expensive than the imported oxide. Cobalt oxide is the most powerful of all the coloring oxides for tinting.

**Decalcomania** – a process of transferring a wet paper print onto the surface of an item. It was made to resemble hand painted work.

**Diaper pattern** – repetitive pattern of small design, often geometric or floral.

**Dragons (ryu)** – a symbol of strength, goodness and good fortune. The Japanese dragon has three claws and was thought to reside in the sky. Clouds, water and lightning often accompany the dragon. The dragon is often portrayed in high relief using the slip trailing method of decoration (moriage).

**Drain mold** – a mold used in making hollow ware. Liquid slip is poured into the mold until the desired thickness of the walls is achieved. The excess clay is then poured out. When the trim starts to shrink away from the mold it is removed.

**Drape mold or flopover mold** – used to make flat bottomed items. Moist clay is rolled out and draped over the mold. It is then pressed firmly into shape.

**Etched gold** – engraving by "biting out by acid" on the pieces.

**Figural** – items having either a relief figure attached for ornamentation to an utilitarian item or the item is a figure that is utilitarian by itself.

**Figurine** – a small molded figure or statuette with no moving parts. It is strictly ornamental and not utilitarian.

**Finial** – the top knob on a cover of an item, used to left the cover off.

**Firing** – the cooking or baking of clay ware.

**Flux** – an ingredient added to glaze to assist in making

the item fire properly. It causes the glaze to melt at a specified temperature.

**Glaze** – composed of silica, alumina and flux and is applied to porcelain pieces. During the firing process the glaze joins together with the clay item to form a glasslike surface. It seals the pores and makes them impervious to liquids.

**Gold trim** – has to be fired at lower temperatures or the gold would sink into the enameled decoration. If overfired the gold becomes discolored.

**Greenware** – clay which has been molded but not fired.

**Hard paste porcelain** – paste meaning the body of substance, porcelain being made from clay using kaolin. This produces a hard translucent body when fired.

**Howo and Hoo bird** – sort of a bird of paradise which resides on earth and is associated with the Empress of Japan. Also see phoenix bird.

**Jasper ware** – see wedgwood.

**Jigger** – a machine resembling a potter's wheel. Soft pliable clay is placed onto a convex revolving mold. As the wheel turns, a template is held against it trimming off the excess clay on the outside. The revolving mold shapes the inside of the item and the template cuts the outside.

**Jolley** – a machine like a jigger only in reverse. The revolving mold is concave and the template forms the inside of the item. The template is lowered inside the revolving mold. The mold forms the outside surface while the template cuts the inside.

**Kaolin** – a highly refractory clay and one of the principal ingredients used in making porcelain. It is a pure white residual clay.

**Kiln** – oven in which pottery is fired.

**Larkin Company**– founded in Buffalo, NY in 1875. This company imported many items manufactured by the Noritake Company and sold them through their mail order catalogs.

**Leather hard clay** – clay which is dry enough to hold its shape but still damp and moist, no longer in a plastic state, also called cheese hard.

**Liquid slip** – clay in a liquid state.

**Luster decoration** – a metallic type of coloring decoration giving an iridescent effect.

**Matte finish** – also referred to as mat and matt. A dull glaze having a low reflectance when fired.

**McKinley Tarrif Act of 1890** – Chapter 1244, Section 6, states "That on and after the first day of March, eighteen hundred and ninety one, all articles of foreign manufacture, such as are usually or ordinarily marked, stamped, branded, or labeled, and all packages containing such or other imported articles, shall, respectively, be plainly marked, stamped, branded, or labeled in legible English words, so as to indicate the country of their origin and unless so marked, stamped, branded, or labeled they shall not be admitted to entry."

**Molds** – contain a cavity in which castings are made. They are generally made from plaster of paris and are used for shaping clay objects. Both liquid and plastic clay may be used. The mold can also be made of clay or rubber, however, plaster was generally used as it absorbed moisture immediately from the clay. Raised ornamentation may also be formed directly in the mold.

**Moriage** – refers to applied clay (slip) relief decoration. This was usually done by slip trailing or hand rolling and shaping the clay on an item.

**Morimura Bros.** – importers of Japanese wares in the United States. It was founded in 1876 in Tokyo and a store was opened in NYC in 1877. The NYC store was closed in 1941.

**Overglaze decoration** – a design is either painted on or a decal applied to an item which already has a fired glazed surface. The article is then refired to make the decoration permanent.

**Paulownia flower** – crest of the Empress of Japan.

**Phoenix bird** – sort of a bird of paradise which resides on earth and is associated with the Empress of Japan. This bird appears to be a cross between a peacock, a pheasant and gamecock. There appear to be many designs for this bird. It is also a symbol to the Japanese of all that is beautiful.

**Plastic clay** – clay in a malleable state, able to be shaped and formed without collapsing.

**Porcelain** – a mixture composed mainly of kaolin and petuntse which is fired at a high temperature and vitrified.

**Potter's wheel** – rotating device on which a ball of plastic clay is placed. The wheel is turned and the potter molds the clay with his hands and is capable of producing cylindrical objects.

**Press mold** – used to make handles, finials, figurines, etc. A two-piece mold into which soft clay is placed. The two pieces are pressed together to form items.

**Relief molded** – the pattern is embossed on the item by the mold in which the article is shaped. These items give the appearance that the pattern is caused by some type of upward pressure from the underside. Collectors often refer to these items as "blown-out."

**Slip** – liquid clay.

**Slip trailing** – a process where liquid clay was applied to porcelain via a rubber tube. It is a form of painting but with clay instead of paint. The slip is often applied quite heavily and gives a thick, raised appearance.

**Solid casting mold** – used for shallow type items such as bowls and plates. In this type of mold the thickness of the walls is determined by the mold and every piece is formed identically. The mold shapes both the inside and the outside of the piece and the thickness of the walls can be controlled.

**Sprigging** – the application of small molded relief decoration to the surface of porcelain by use of liquid clay as in Jasper ware.

**Sprig mold** – a one-piece mold used in making ornaments. Clay is fitted or poured into a mold which is incised with a design. Only one side is molded and the exposed side becomes the back of the finished item.

**Taisho** – name of period reigned over by Emperor Yoshihito in Japan from 1912-1926. It means great peace.

**Ultraviolet lamp** – lamp used to detect cracks and hidden repairs on items.

**Underglaze decoration** – this type of decoration is applied on bisque china (fired once), then the item is glazed and fired again.

**Wedgwood** – term used to refer to pieces which attempt to imitate Josiah Wedgwood's Jasper ware. The items generally have a light blue or green background. White clay slip was usually trailed onto the background color of the item by use of tubing to form the pattern. The sprigging technique was employed on other pieces.

**Yoshihito** – Emperor of Japan from 1912-26. He took the name of Taisho which meant great peace.

# Bibliography

Arwas, Victor, *Art Deco Sculpture*, St. Martin's Press, New York, 1975.

Butler Bros. catalogs, #'s 2395, 2538, 2849, 3062, 4806.

Duncan Alastair, *The Encyclopedia of Art Deco*, Quarto Publishing, London, 1988.

Hillier, Bevis, *Art Deco of the Twenties and Thirties*, Schocken Books, New York, 1985.

Klein, Dan, McClelland, Nance, A., Haslam, Malcolm, *In the Deco Style*, Rizzoli International Publications, Inc, New York, 1986.

Larkin catalogs, #'s 92, 96, 98, 100.

McClinton, Katherine, Morrison, *Art Deco, A Guide for Collectors*, Clarkson N. Potter, Inc. New York, 1972.

Van Patten, Joan, F., *The Collector's Encyclopedia of Nippon Porcelain*, Collector Books, Paducah, KY, 1979.

Van Patten, Joan, F., *The Collector's Encyclopedia of Nippon Porcelain, Series II*, Collector Books, Paducah, KY, 1982.

Van Patten, Joan, F., *The Collector's Encyclopedia of Nippon, Series III*, Collector Books, Paducah, KY, 1986.

Van Patten, Joan, F., *The Collector's Encyclopedia of Noritake*, Collector Books, Paducah, KY, 1986.

Weber, Eva, *Art Deco in America*, Bison Books, New York, 1985.

# Other Books by Joan Van Patten

Collector's Encyclopedia of Nippon .............................................$19.95

Collector's Encyclopedia of Nippon, Second Series ....................$24.95

Collector's Encyclopedia of Nippon, Third Series.......................$24.95

Nippon Porcelain Price Guide .......................................................$7.95

Collector's Encyclopedia of Noritake.............................................$19.95

# Books on Antiques and Collectibles

This is only a partial listing of the books on antiques that are available from Collector Books. All books are well illustrated and contain current values. Most of the following books are available from your local book seller, antique dealer, or public library. If you are unable to locate certain titles in your area, you may order by mail from COLLECTOR BOOKS, P.O. Box 3009, Paducah, KY 42002-3009. Customers with Visa or MasterCard may phone in orders from 8:00 – 4:00 CST, M – F – Toll Free 1-800-626-5420. Add $2.00 for postage for the first book ordered and $0.30 for each additional book. Include item number, title, and price when ordering. Allow 14 to 21 days for delivery.

## BOOKS ON GLASS AND POTTERY

| | | |
|---|---|---|
| 1810 | American Art Glass, Shuman | $29.95 |
| 2016 | Bedroom & Bathroom Glassware of the Depression Years | $19.95 |
| 1312 | Blue & White Stoneware, McNerney | $9.95 |
| 1959 | Blue Willow, 2nd Ed., Gaston | $14.95 |
| 3719 | Coll. Glassware from the 40's, 50's, 60's, 2nd Ed., Florence | $19.95 |
| 3311 | Collecting Yellow Ware – Id. & Value Gd., McAllister | $16.95 |
| 2352 | Collector's Ency. of Akro Agate Glassware, Florence | $14.95 |
| 1373 | Collector's Ency. of American Dinnerware, Cunningham | 24.95 |
| 2272 | Collector's Ency. of California Pottery, Chipman | $24.95 |
| 3312 | Collector's Ency. of Children's Dishes, Whitmyer | $19.95 |
| 2133 | Collector's Ency. of Cookie Jars, Roerig | $24.95 |
| 3724 | Collector's Ency. of Depression Glass, 11th Ed., Florence | $19.95 |
| 2209 | Collector's Ency. of Fiesta, 7th Ed., Huxford | $19.95 |
| 1439 | Collector's Ency. of Flow Blue China, Gaston | $19.95 |
| 1915 | Collector's Ency. of Hall China, 2nd Ed., Whitmyer | $19.95 |
| 2334 | Collector's Ency. of Majolica Pottery, Katz-Marks | $19.95 |
| 1358 | Collector's Ency. of McCoy Pottery, Huxford | $19.95 |
| 3313 | Collector's Ency. of Niloak, Gifford | $19.95 |
| 1039 | Collector's Ency. of Nippon Porcelain I, Van Patten | $19.95 |
| 2089 | Collector's Ency. of Nippon Porcelain II, Van Patten | $24.95 |
| 1665 | Collector's Ency. of Nippon Porcelain III, Van Patten | $24.95 |
| 1447 | Collector's Ency. of Noritake, 1st Series, Van Patten | $19.95 |
| 1034 | Collector's Ency. of Roseville Pottery, Huxford | $19.95 |
| 1035 | Collector's Ency. of Roseville Pottery, 2nd Ed., Huxford | $19.95 |
| 3314 | Collector's Ency. of Van Briggle Art Pottery, Sasicki | $24.95 |
| 3433 | Collector's Guide To Harker Pottery - U.S.A., Colbert | $17.95 |
| 2339 | Collector's Guide to Shawnee Pottery, Vanderbilt | $19.95 |
| 1425 | Cookie Jars, Westfall | $9.95 |
| 3440 | Cookie Jars, Book II, Westfall | $19.95 |
| 2275 | Czechoslovakian Glass & Collectibles, Barta | $16.95 |
| 3315 | Elegant Glassware of the Depression Era, 5th Ed., Florence | $19.95 |
| 3318 | Glass Animals of the Depression Era, Garmon & Spencer | $19.95 |
| 2024 | Kitchen Glassware of the Depression Years, 4th Ed., Florence | $19.95 |
| 3322 | Pocket Guide to Depression Glass, 8th Ed., Florence | $9.95 |
| 1670 | Red Wing Collectibles, DePasquale | $9.95 |
| 1440 | Red Wing Stoneware, DePasquale | $9.95 |
| 1958 | So. Potteries Blue Ridge Dinnerware, 3rd Ed., Newbound | $14.95 |
| 3739 | Standard Carnival Glass, 4th Ed., Edwards | $24.95 |
| 1848 | Very Rare Glassware of the Depression Years, Florence | $24.95 |
| 2140 | Very Rare Glassware of the Depression Years, Second Series | $24.95 |
| 3326 | Very Rare Glassware of the Depression Years, Third Series | $24.95 |
| 3327 | Watt Pottery – Identification & Value Guide, Morris | $19.95 |
| 2224 | World of Salt Shakers, 2nd Ed., Lechner | $24.95 |

## BOOKS ON DOLLS & TOYS

| | | |
|---|---|---|
| 2079 | Barbie Fashion, Vol. 1, 1959-1967, Eames | $24.95 |
| 3310 | Black Dolls – 1820 - 1991 – Id. & Value Guide, Perkins | $17.95 |
| 1514 | Character Toys & Collectibles, 1st Series, Longest | $19.95 |
| 1750 | Character Toys & Collectibles, 2nd Series, Longest | $19.95 |
| 1529 | Collector's Ency. of Barbie Dolls, DeWein | $19.95 |
| 2338 | Collector's Ency. of Disneyana, Longest & Stern | $24.95 |
| 3441 | Madame Alexander Price Guide #18, Smith | $9.95 |
| 1540 | Modern Toys, 1930 - 1980, Baker | $19.95 |
| 3442 | Patricia Smith's Doll Values – Antique to Modern, 9th ed | $12.95 |
| 1886 | Stern's Guide to Disney | $14.95 |

| | | |
|---|---|---|
| 2139 | Stern's Guide to Disney, 2nd Series | $14.95 |
| 1513 | Teddy Bears & Steiff Animals, Mandel | $9.95 |
| 1817 | Teddy Bears & Steiff Animals, 2nd Series, Mandel | $19.95 |
| 2084 | Teddy Bears, Annalees & Steiff Animals, 3rd Series, Mandel | $19.95 |
| 2028 | Toys, Antique & Collectible, Longest | $14.95 |
| 1808 | Wonder of Barbie, Manos | $9.95 |
| 1430 | World of Barbie Dolls, Manos | $9.95 |

## OTHER COLLECTIBLES

| | | |
|---|---|---|
| 1457 | American Oak Furniture, McNerney | $9.95 |
| 2269 | Antique Brass & Copper, Gaston | $16.95 |
| 2333 | Antique & Collectible Marbles, 3rd Ed., Grist | $9.95 |
| 1712 | Antique & Collectible Thimbles, Mathis | $19.95 |
| 1748 | Antique Purses, Holiner | $19.95 |
| 1868 | Antique Tools, Our American Heritage, McNerney | $9.95 |
| 1426 | Arrowheads & Projectile Points, Hothem | $7.95 |
| 1278 | Art Nouveau & Art Deco Jewelry, Baker | $9.95 |
| 1714 | Black Collectibles, Gibbs | $19.95 |
| 1128 | Bottle Pricing Guide, 3rd Ed., Cleveland | $7.95 |
| 1752 | Christmas Ornaments, Johnston | $19.95 |
| 2132 | Collector's Ency. of American Furniture, Vol. I, Swedberg | $24.95 |
| 2271 | Collector's Ency. of American Furniture, Vol. II, Swedberg | $24.95 |
| 2018 | Collector's Ency. of Granite Ware, Greguire | $24.95 |
| 3430 | Coll. Ency. of Granite Ware, Book 2, Greguire | $24.95 |
| 2083 | Collector's Ency. of Russel Wright Designs, Kerr | $19.95 |
| 2337 | Collector's Guide to Decoys, Book II, Huxford | $16.95 |
| 2340 | Collector's Guide to Easter Collectibles, Burnett | $16.95 |
| 1441 | Collector's Guide to Post Cards, Wood | $9.95 |
| 2276 | Decoys, Kangas | $24.95 |
| 1629 | Doorstops – Id. & Values, Bertoia | $9.95 |
| 1716 | Fifty Years of Fashion Jewelry, Baker | $19.95 |
| 3316 | Flea Market Trader, 8th Ed., Huxford | $9.95 |
| 3317 | Florence's Standard Baseball Card Price Gd., 5th Ed. | $9.95 |
| 1755 | Furniture of the Depression Era, Swedberg | $19.95 |
| 3436 | Grist's Big Book of Marbles, Everett Grist | $19.95 |
| 2278 | Grist's Machine Made & Contemporary Marbles | $9.95 |
| 1424 | Hatpins & Hatpin Holders, Baker | $9.95 |
| 3319 | Huxford's Collectible Advertising – Id. & Value Gd. | $17.95 |
| 3439 | Huxford's Old Book Value Guide, 5th Ed. | $19.95 |
| 1181 | 100 Years of Collectible Jewelry, Baker | $9.95 |
| 2023 | Keen Kutter Collectibles, 2nd Ed., Heuring | $14.95 |
| 2216 | Kitchen Antiques – 1790 - 1940, McNerney | $14.95 |
| 3320 | Modern Guns – Id. & Val. Gd., 9th Ed., Quertermous | $12.95 |
| 1965 | Pine Furniture, Our American Heritage, McNerney | $14.95 |
| 3321 | Ornamental & Figural Nutcrackers, Rittenhouse | $16.95 |
| 2026 | Railroad Collectibles, 4th Ed., Baker | $14.95 |
| 1632 | Salt & Pepper Shakers, Guarnaccia | $9.95 |
| 1888 | Salt & Pepper Shakers II, Guarnaccia | $14.95 |
| 2220 | Salt & Pepper Shakers III, Guarnaccia | $14.95 |
| 3443 | Salt & Pepper Shakers IV, Guarnaccia | $18.95 |
| 3737 | Schroeder's Antiques Price Guide, 12th Ed. | $12.95 |
| 2096 | Silverplated Flatware, 4th Ed., Hagan | $14.95 |
| 3325 | Standard Knife Collector's Guide, 2nd Ed., Stewart | $12.95 |
| 2348 | 20th Century Fashionable Plastic Jewelry, Baker | $19.95 |
| 3444 | Wanted To Buy, 4th Ed. | $9.95 |